Once Upon a Line

Token exchange at Smallbrook Junction with the smiling Signalman Vic Hailes and the driver of No. 33 *Bembridge* on 11 June 1966.

John Goss

Once Upon a Line

Reminiscences of the Isle of Wight Railways

Edited by

Andrew Britton

Volume Two

Oxford Publishing Company

Typeset by: Aquarius Typesetting Services,
New Milton, Hants.

Printed in Great Britain by:
Netherwood Dalton & Co. Ltd., Huddersfield, Yorks.

DEDICATION

This book is dedicated to the memory of Admiral of the Fleet Earl Mountbatten of Burma, KG, PC, Governor and Lord Lieutenant of the Isle of Wight, who took a keen interest in the Island railways, which have had associations with the Royal Family dating back to the times of Her Majesty Queen Victoria. As a railway enthusiast, Earl Mountbatten was delighted to visit the Isle of Wight Steam Railway which he predicted would be a major Island tourist attraction and a fitting tribute to those who served on it in bygone days — many of whom have contributed to the *Once Upon A Line* books.

Published by:
Oxford Publishing Co.
Link House
West Street
POOLE, Dorset

ACKNOWLEDGEMENTS

Never before in my life have I come across so many kind and generous people as those with whom I have come into contact in connection with the *Once Upon A Line* books. They have helped me in different ways in compiling this book and the first volume, by supplying information as evidence to support contributors' anecdotes, offering valuable advice and giving much encouragement.

My thanks must go firstly to five very special people who have kept me on the right lines — my wife Annette, my mother and father, Dick Blenkinsop, and Beth Young of Blandford Press.

A book of this kind greatly benefits from some unique illustrations which help bring the text to life, and for their assistance in this essential task I would like to record my thanks to the following people: John Goss, Timothy P. Cooper, George Hunt, Dr Gerald Siviour, H. Peter Mason, Ron Childs, Dr John Mackett, Tim Genower, R. J. Blenkinsop, Mike Esau, Ian Whitlam, Syd Dennett, Anthony E. Bennett, Bob Burroughs, the Wight Locomotive Society/A. B. MacLeod Collection, British Railways Board (Southern Region), Peter J. Relf, Bob Church, Jim Hewitt, Eric Bruton, Ray Draper, Sid Newberry, the late Bill Miller, Portsmouth Newspapers Ltd., and John A. Britton.

The tickets pictured in this book were placed at my disposal by Timothy P. Cooper and Stephen Johnson. Eventually the original tickets from both collections will be placed on display at the Isle of Wight Steam Railway Museum. Only a representative selection of these tickets has been reproduced in this volume, and to appreciate the collection in its entirety would require a book in its own right!

Special mention must be made of those people who have opened their homes to me during the research for this book, namely, Mike 'Chuff' Downer, Ian Wightmore, Richard Newman, and Eddie Prangnell. Better food and hospitality could not be found in a five star hotel!

Considerable assistance during the research stage was also given by the Isle of Wight Steam Railway, who generously hosted reunions of serving and retired railway staff. Not only have these greatly assisted me, but they have also brought considerable enjoyment to the railway staff and their families. To the volunteers at Haven Street who have given so much of their valuable time to these functions may I offer my sincere thanks. Likewise, much help in tracing contributors has been given by newspapers, local radio, and television — my thanks for putting up with the many telephone calls and letters.

The handwritten manuscript was typed up by those faithful stalwarts Mrs Barber, Mrs Checketts, Wendy Adams and my wife.

My thanks must also go to artist Barry Walding for his delightful painting on the front cover of this book and also to Bryan Hicks who kindly supplied the colour print which appears on the back cover.

Finally, my deepest gratitude goes to Jimmy E. James whose cartoon drawings are a unique first hand record of the Island railways. Their reproduction in this book has been eagerly awaited by Island railway staff and railway enthusiasts alike.

CONTENTS

Foreword

I know it had been Andrew Britton's intention to ask my father to write the Foreword to this second volume of his *Once Upon A Line* series but since this is now tragically impossible the invitation has kindly been extended to me — although I have no expertise on the subject! However I do have a real love of trains which are my preferred method of travel and full of interest and excitement. Last year I travelled alone across the breadth of Canada on the Canadian Pacific from Vancouver to New Brunswick (with a break in Montreal) a fascinating 6-day journey. I have also been lucky enough to travel the Nullabor Plain — to Sydney; and in South Africa from Johannesburg to the Cape on the Blue Train. In India I journeyed from Delhi to Kashmir by rail and in Europe I have been from London to Venice on the Orient Express and also from Helsinki to Moscow and back by Warsaw.

I was thrilled by all these marvellous long journeys, but I also love a much shorter journey I sometimes take (often with children or grandchildren) on my neighbouring Romney, Hythe and Dymchurch miniature

steam railway in Kent. I have had the great pleasure of taking the Queen and Prince Philip with a very excited Prince Charles and Princess Anne for a run on that line, as well as my father who was very keen on it.

Certainly my father always found railways very exciting and I was so very pleased when, in 1980, British Rail named three locomotives *Mountbatten of Burma, Broadlands* and *Burma Star* in his memory (which I always hope to encounter on my travels!) I know what a special interest he took in the Isle of Wight Steam Railway and how much he enjoyed his visit to the Steam Railway Museum in 1976 and a journey between Haven Street and Wootton when he took over the controls of the vintage steam engine and thoroughly enjoyed himself.

I am sure it is well known what a deep interest and love my father had for The Island of which he felt so privileged to be both Governor and Lord Lieutenant. I know he would have been pleased that its remarkable and historic steam railways should have been so admirably recorded and so many memories of it immortalised for future generations by Andrew Britton.

Countess Mountbatten of Burma
Kent,
1984

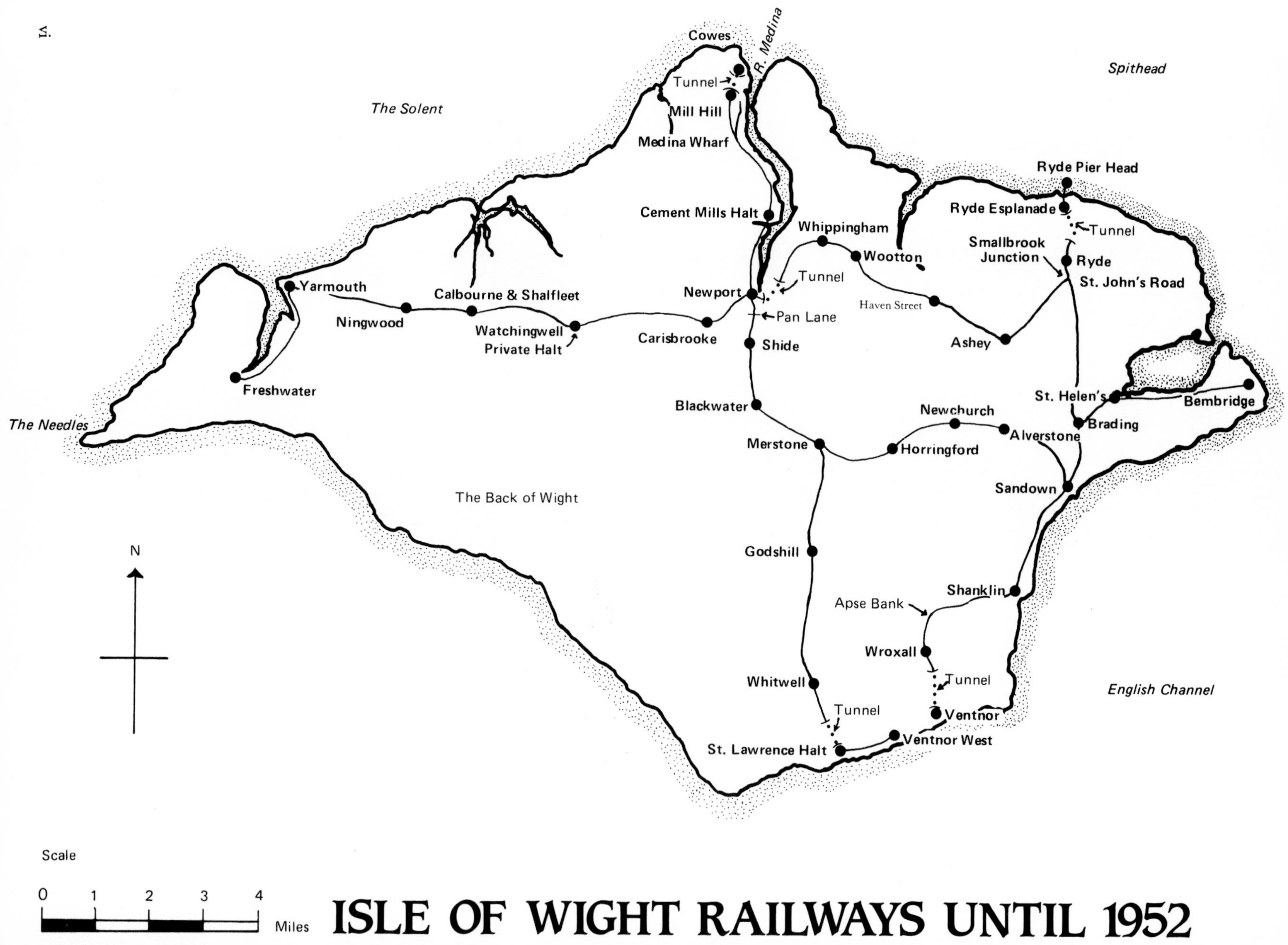

ISLE OF WIGHT RAILWAYS UNTIL 1952

Spithead

English Channel

Ryde Pier Head
Ryde Esplanade
Smallbrook Junction
Ryde
St. John's Road
Tunnel
Bembridge
Brading
St. Helen's
Alverstone
Sandown
Ashey
Newchurch
Horringford
Shanklin
Wootton
Haven Street
Whippingham
Tunnel
Pan Lane
Shide
Merstone
Godshill
Apse Bank
Wroxall
Tunnel
Ventnor
Ventnor West
Whitwell
Tunnel
St. Lawrence Halt

R. Medina
Cowes
Tunnel
Mill Hill
Medina Wharf
Cement Mills Halt
Newport
Carisbrooke
Blackwater

Watchingwell
Private Halt
Calbourne & Shalfleet
The Back of Wight

The Solent

Yarmouth
Ningwood
Freshwater

The Needles

N

Scale

0   1   2   3   4

Miles

vi

PREFACE

Following on from *Once Upon A Line* Volume One which dealt with the stories of footplate staff, guards, works staff, and the Permanent Way Department, this second volume in the series covers the stories of station staff and signalmen. It has been very difficult to separate the different departments of the railways as there was considerable overlap and sharing of responsibilities.

In this integrated railway network, where the seasonal traffic variation caused problems, the smooth and efficient working of station staff, signalmen and related services was the lynch pin of the successful operation of the system. Ryde Pier Head Station on a busy summer Saturday left one gasping at the magnitude of the task. At the peak period of the day, the station concourse would appear busier than London Waterloo, with the coming and going of thousands of holidaymakers. Yet despite this seemingly impossible situation, trains and boats departed on time and one was left wondering how the staff managed to cope so efficiently. A sense of loyalty, responsibility and hard work with careful timetabling was the answer. The staff involved accepted the challenge and proved their metal.

In this island is to be found some of the most delightful scenery in the British Isles and within this environment the attractive Isle of Wight stations, signalboxes and lineside railway furniture blended well. The character and individuality of the railway staff reflected the uniqueness of the system, but like most railway staff on other railways they were friendly, helpful, intensely loyal — sometimes a little parochial.

An appendix which will interest the historians contains the War Incidents File. It is now declassified information and can be studied for the first time. It substantiates a number of stories contained in Volume One and in this book. These records highlight the bravery displayed by Isle of Wight staff under enemy attack in World War II. The Royal Family always expressed considerable interest in the Isle of Wight railways — indeed a contributor to this volume mentions that Whippingham Station was built at the express wish of Her Majesty Queen Victoria. This interest has been maintained throughout the years and the late Earl Mountbatten of Burma was certainly a fan of steam railways: when Governor of The Isle of Wight he took the opportunity to visit the preserved section of the Island railways at Haven Street. This was on Thursday 26 January 1976 when he went for a ride on a restored working steam train between Haven Street and Wootton. It is with great pleasure that I remember the Earl Mountbatten inspecting the Royal Train and then climbing up on to the footplate of engine No. 24 *Calbourne*. After a brief conversation with Driver Ray Maxfield and Fireman Len Pullinger, Earl Mountbatten took over the controls and became an engine driver. The Earl later confessed to me that he was a railway enthusiast and enjoyed the engine smells of hot oil and steam. It was obvious to all that he enjoyed this visit immensely.

Earl Mountbaten was no stranger to railway practice and was knowledgeable about other aspects of railway service, which he acquired during World War II. It is thus very appropriate, and I am very grateful, that the Countess Mountbatten of Burma has graciously consented to write the Foreword to *Once Upon A Line* Volume Two.

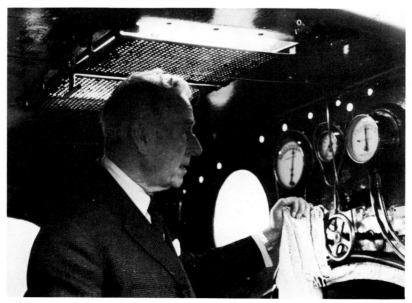

Earl Mountbatten prepares to ease the regulator of No. 24 *Calbourne* open as he drives his Royal Train away from Haven Street. The stance of a real engineman.

Peter J. Relf

Six days unlimited travel in the ISLE OF WIGHT with HOLIDAY RUNABOUT TICKETS

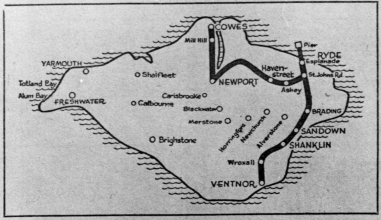

During 1963 Holiday Runabout Tickets in the Isle of Wight will be obtainable from 28th April to 25th October, available for six days, starting any day from SUNDAY to FRIDAY (but **not** valid on Saturdays)

They can be purchased at stations in the island for travel on any train between stations on the above map.

For the assistance of Holders of these tickets a time table of rail services (Sundays to Fridays) for the period 17th June to 8th September 1963 is given in this folder.

10/-
SECOND CLASS

15/- FIRST CLASS

CHILDREN HALF PRICE
(3 years and under 14)

BICYCLE	..	..	::	::	::	
DOG		..	::	::	::	5/-
INVALID CHAIR	..	..	::	::	::	
(Not folded) under 60 lb. in weight						
PRAM *(Not folded)*						
TANDEM	..	..	::	::	::	7/6

SOUTHERN
BRITISH RAILWAYS

Published by the Southern Region of British Railways   AD9503/A45/4263/BR35008/1

Printed in Great Britain by Stafford & Co. Ltd., Netherfield, Nottingham

Chapter One ~ The Ryde Pier Head-Ventnor Line

Mrs Hilda Smith

Ryde Pier Head Station was nearly half a mile out to sea, with paddle steamers such as *Ryde, Sandown* and *Whippingham* ferrying tourists to and from Portsmouth every twenty minutes. During the steam era there were connecting trains with the boats for the Cowes and Ventnor lines, and the Pier Head was the main gateway to the Isle of Wight.

I remember the first week I started work at Ryde Pier Head in 1940 during the early part of World War II. As I travelled up the Pier, I noticed that there were two anti-aircraft guns. Their crews were billeted in the Pier Head Pavilion, while the Royal Navy had commandeered the shop. On my first day the anti-aircraft guns opened up on a hit and run German plane which machine gunned the Pier. During the attack there was a train waiting in the station and they were unloading milk churns. The porter dived under the train whilst the Booking Office clerk stuck his head in the safe — it was just as well, as a bullet hit the door ricocheting on to the wall. We all had a very lucky escape that memorable first day.

As I worked in the buffet, I soon got to know all the Island railwaymen. In fact, I later married the ticket collector at the Pier and my brother was a driver until the closure of the Cowes and Ventnor lines in 1966. Many interesting and famous people including film stars and singers travelled on the Island trains in those days, and they would often visit the buffet. When Mr. Herbert Morrison was a member of the Government he called in one Christmas and was full of praise for the decorations. All the staff used to help with the tree and Christmas decorations — we took a tremendous pride in Ryde Pier Head Station.

Just after the War, when the beaches were opened around the Island again, the visitors began to return. Some Saturdays at the height of the summer season, I have seen queues of people stretching all the way down to the Pier. Sometimes there would be up to 60,000 people per day! Passengers would arrive at the Pier Head Station and then have to walk back down the Pier towards the Esplanade Station to join the back of the queue. There don't seem to be so many tourists about now that the lines have closed.

Reg L. Aylward

In January 1912 I began my apprenticeship at Ryde St. John's Road Works. World War I interrupted my railway career, and I joined the Royal Flying Corps, later to become the RAF. Upon returning to the 'Land Fit for Heroes' after the War, I discovered that things had changed for the worse. There was no job waiting for me at Ryde Works, so I had five years on the footplate as a fireman. The Southern Railway then completed electrifying the Waterloo – Portsmouth line and many junior enginemen were made redundant. I was one of them. There was no dole then, so I had to take a job as boiler washer at Newport Shed.

August Bank Holiday 1928 brought a stroke of luck for me when one of the old electric tram drivers on Ryde Pier tramway had a mishap. I was then called upon to take over driving the trams which ran parallel to the main railway line between the Pier Head and Esplanade stations. The previous November two Drewry petrol cars had arrived for use on the tramway. They came by night and were jacked up over the Esplanade on to the railway. We drove the trams to the Pier Head sitting at the rear of the tram set, and we had to judge the distance from the end of the line. Well, on this Bank Holiday the inevitable happened and the driver overran at some speed and wrecked the tram.

The pay was very poor, and we only survived by working on summer Sundays. During the summer months we used to have Works' parties visiting the Island for the day. I remember one crowd came down from a cigarette firm. They were rather 'merry' on the tram, and I felt very sorry for the young lad who was conducting. The girls practically cornered him.

It was a very monotonous job backwards and forwards on the Pier, with only the pleasure of seeing liners passing, so I was glad to finish my last days as a ticket collector at the Esplanade Station.

Victor Arthur Verdun Lacey

My father was signalman at Ryde St. John's signal-box, and it soon became evident when I left school in March 1930 at the age of fourteen, that I would follow

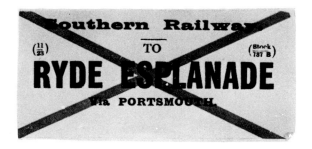

Caught in the act of fishing at Ryde Pier Head Station! I wonder what Messrs. Alan Kellaway, Jack Daish, and George Sherlock, managed to catch for their suppers?

Ron H. Childs

'Gateway to the Isle of Wight' No. 21 *Sandown* prepares to depart for Ventnor from Ryde Pier Head in July 1965. Ryde Pier Head Station was unique in this country. Several railway stations were located over water but none actually right out 'at sea'. The first station, built in 1879, was jointly owned by the LSWR and LBSCR, but used by trains of the independent Central and Isle of Wight Railway Companies. In 1933 the station was completely remodelled and further changes were made in 1966 and 1967. Four platforms were provided in steam days, with apron roofs — two usually dealing with arrivals and two with departures. A large water tank, seen here, was provided at the end of platforms 1 and 2, and a smaller column at the end of platforms 3 and 4. On the west side of the station a high wooden wall shut off the sea, but to the east only low ornamental railings were provided. In summer the platforms were packed with holidaymakers, but on a cold winter's day Ryde Pier Head Station could be almost deserted, a bleak spot indeed. Following the fall of France in 1940 a young army officer, hearing that piers along the south coast were to be destroyed or cut in half to foil enemy landings, attempted to blow up Ryde Pier. He instructed his men to plant high explosive charges along the Pier and was about to evacuate all personnel when railway officials managed to apprehend him before handing him over to a higher authority!

Dr Gerald R. Siviour

'Oh, it's so nice to be beside the sea-side!' especially when steam trains travel up and down Ryde Pier.

R. J. Blenkinsop

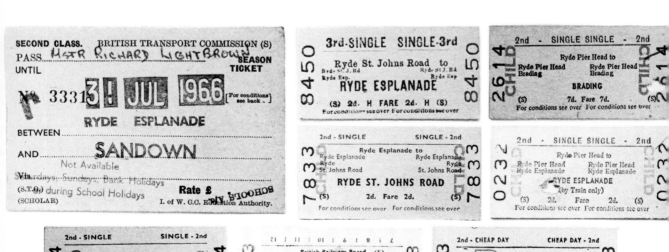

No. 31 *Chale* approaches Ryde Esplanade with a train for Cowes in 1931. Here the line curved very sharply through the two platforms which were partly built on land and partly over the sea. Note the lower quadrant signals and the delightful advertisement signs — such a characteristic part of the Island stations.

George H Hunt

Ryde Pier Gates, 1930, by Jimmy James

him in a career on the Island Railways. The times were drifting into the 1930s economic slump; however, I started as a temporary tram conductor for the summer of 1930. There were two sets of two-car trams, a petrol-driven Drewry car with a trailer of the Victorian era, holding over 200 passengers when fully laden. The conductor was expected to get through this lot in three minutes, and very often if the driver did not want to hang about it had to be one and a half minutes. When you got to the end of the journey the conductor had to be first off, to rush to the exit with the intention of collecting all the tickets and fares that had been missed. August Bank Holiday was a teaser; we were on the go all day. The fare was 1½d adult single; no return. To get from trailer to Drewry car and vice versa, you had to climb over the ends — one slip and you could be in the sea below the pier. This did happen to one conductor; luckily he missed the cross supports of the track and went down in the drink. Another hazard of climbing over was that if your cash bag swung around and hit your thigh, very

often a bunch of fifty tickets and maybe some cash would fall in the drink. With no record, you were short and there was no other way but to be stopped the short-fall out of your wages.

At the end of the summer service I had to stand off, but very soon a vacancy turned up at the C.M.E and Locomotive Offices at Ryde Works for an office boy. I started on Thursday, 13 November 1930 (which became my service date), and the clerk remarked it was my lucky day. Well, the first bit of luck was that I had to work Thursday, Friday and Saturday for nothing — this was the condition of becoming permanent. So after earning 16 shillings a week plus overtime, Sundays etc. I had to knuckle back to 5 shillings a week less fourpence insurance, and no overtime or Sunday work.

The next stage was at sixteen when I was too old for this job, so now at the depth of the national economic depression, I had to take a temporary parcel porter post at Ryde St. John's Road. Here at summer weekends the PLA (Passenger Luggage in Advance) would pile up to

No. 14 *Fishbourne* pulls away from Ryde Esplanade Station with a train for Newport and Cowes.

R. J. Blenkinsop

An original small bunkered '02' prepares to depart from Ryde Esplanade Station with a Ryde Pier Head – Sandown train, in 1929. From here the line dipped steeply at a gradient of 1:50 to the tunnel under the Esplanade. Note the charabanc touring coaches awaiting the holidaymakers.

George H. Hunt

The line emerged from the Esplanade Tunnel on a rising gradient of 1:66 near Simeon Street. Beyond the tunnel the line passed the gas works — the remains of which are pictured complete with disused siding.

R. J. Blenkinsop

Ryde St. John's Road Station in the autumn of 1929. The signal box at the south end of the up platform is of interest in that it was formerly in service at Waterloo Junction on the SECR.

George H. Hunt

roof height for the resort station.

With the end of the 1932 summer service, I was stood off again for the winter season. The next summer they sent for me again at Ryde St. John's Road, but this time for 'fish, meat and fruit'. The fish arrived at the station in hundred weight boxes, meat was hind quarters, and fruit was in tons. All had to be man-handled. There were 17-gallon churns of milk as well. The season passed all too quickly, and the following March, 1934, they called me back, this time for a newly invented post.

The branch line between Merstone Junction (on the Newport – Sandown Road) and Ventnor West was to run without a guard during the winter timetable late shift, but in his place was to be a junior parcel porter, this turned out to be me. The first week I had to learn the job, with my opposite number on the early turn at Newport Parcel Office, and late turn on the branch. Our duties there were to issue and collect tickets, do parcel work on the train for the halts involved, and clean the train inside out.

One cold November night on the Ventnor West Branch on the junior parcel porter duty, we had a ram to deliver to Whitwell last trip. There was £1 something to collect from the farmer. The last journey was to return to Merstone where the stock was to be berthed into a siding, and then light engine to Newport. On this occasion, it turned out happily enough, the farmer was there, with the correct money down to the last halfpenny. But I had had visions of taking that ram all the way back to Newport on the engine footplate!

When summer came, it was Newport Parcel Office for me, and my opposite number went to Sandown Parcel Office. Winter arrived, and it was back to the Ventor West Branch, but by chance a vacancy turned up at St. Helen's on the Bembridge Branch, which I was lucky enough to obtain.

St. Helen's was an interesting station, as it gave you the opportunity of learning all aspects of railway work with the exception of signalling (this branch was run on a 'Key Token — one Engine In Steam' system). At St. Helen's, Chaplins, a local firm, contributed to the goods traffic considerably. This was brought in by boat from the mainland and loaded into box wagons to be labelled, sorted and despatched by the 'mid-day' goods but it was often after dark that it got away, due to the volume of goods. When shunting was involved on the quay we had to operate level crossing gates across the main road to Bembridge, sometimes until midnight according to the amount of work involved. Remember, at this stage in my career I was still only a junior parcel porter at a station!

Whilst based at Newport, I had another unusual job, probably the most unlikely job on any railway company in Britain. I was sent to relieve another junior parcel porter who was on holiday for a week, and this involved being a spy. The Southern Railway Company had an air service running between Cowes, Ryde and Heston, whereas an opposition service ran between Cowes, Ryde and Croydon. My task was to spy on what luggage and number of passengers boarded and alighted from the opposition's plane. This was a great job in fine weather, but when it rained it was miserable, as the only place we could get a clear view was on the main road or public enclosure which was an area surrounded by chestnut fencing. However, there were exceptional views when 'Sir Alan Cobham's Air Circus' arrived.

March 1937 saw my return to Ryde St. John's Road as a leading porter at just one farthing an hour more than a porter received. I saw all the War years there. One drizzly night during wintertime in the early years of the War, I recall the platforms being chocabloc with passengers returning home from Cowes and the boat building yards awaiting connections with the Ventnor line. We heard quite suddenly some enemy aeroplanes passing overhead, and one released a stick of eight bombs across the down line, but the last one hit the middle track just a few yards from the station, with a train approaching. The driver saw the bomb explode but could not stop in time and the locomotive entered the bomb crater. Station staff managed to get all the passengers out of the train, and guided them to the air raid shelter. There was just one casualty, not serious.

The year 1943 saw me as a signalman at Ryde St. John's Road Box. This was a unique occurrence in that my father was still signalman there. However, as I was always used to being out of doors, this job didn't really suit me. So in 1945 I applied to become a goods guard. My story as a guard is told in Volume One of *Once Upon a Line*.

Ted Bowers

Whilst working at St. John's Road as the station master's clerk, I walked out on the platform and witnessed an extraordinary set of events. George Sherlock, one of the porters, was raising the platform indicators. After the train left for Ventnor he lowered the board just as Stationmaster Bert Smith was passing. The wooden board inscribed 'Next train—Brading, Sandown, Shanklin, Wroxall and Ventnor' hit him right on the head, knocking him out. The next morning poor George received the biggest carpeting you can imagine!

Les Allen

I recall a train pulling in from Ventnor when I was station foreman at St. John's Road, Ryde. A lady looked rather distressed as she alighted from the train, so I approached her and asked if I could be of any assistance. 'Perhaps you can help my husband. He's lost his teeth.' So I asked where he had left them. 'He didn't leave them; they left him as he was looking out of the window at the field with the water pipe,' the lady replied. We walked back along the line towards Smallbrook and sure enough we found them.

As station foreman at St. John's Road it was my job to make up the trains: six carriages for the Ventnor Line and four or five for the Cowes Line. The works staff came across one day for a routine examination of the carriage stock and discovered a defect in a wheel so they sent for the boffins from Headquarters. Presently they arrived to carry out a full examination of the carriage wheel with an ultrasonic machine. They confirmed that the wheel was faulty and painted white marks on the wheels showing the carriage was 'out-of-use—not to be moved'. 'While we are here we will check over the rest of the stock,' said the helpful examiner. I returned from lunch in the afternoon to be greeted by Bob Sweetman, who was foreman over the Ryde Works. 'You've got some trouble over there, we've found six more defective carriages,' Bob said. By Saturday, we had so many withdrawn carriages we could only turn out three coach trains on the Ventnor Road and two coach trains on the Cowes Road, so I sent for the boss Mr Gardiner. He sent for another ultrasonic machine,

No. 28 *Ashey* shunting stock at Ryde St. John's Road, in preparation for the 6.46a.m. to Ventnor on 10 July 1965.

John Goss

16

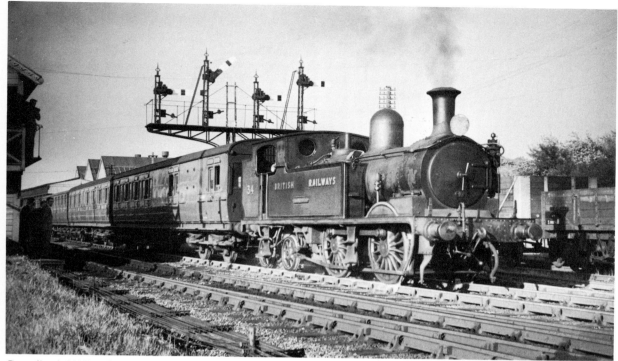

Green liveried '02' tank No. 34 *Newport* gets away smartly with a train for Ventnor on Sunday 18 May 1952. At the time the picture was taken, Smallbrook Junction Signalbox was closed for the winter and the lines between St. John's Road and Smallbrook were operated as two parallel single lines.

Eric D. Bruton

Station Foreman Les Allen on the footplate of the last Island 'E1', No. 4 *Wroxall*, on 4 March 1961. If a train spotter hadn't been kicked out of Ryde St. John's Shed by Foreman Allen he hadn't lived!

H. Peter Mason

and it was found that the original technical wonder was at fault. The red faced boys from the works spent the rest of the morning painting out their white markings on the wheels.

Some years ago, before the closure of the Sandown – Newport Line in the mid 1950s I witnessed a very amusing incident from St. John's Road Station platform. I heard some shunting going on and looked round to see an engine being pushed back into Ryde Works for a major overhaul. Usually, engines entered the workshops bogie first, but this particular locomotive had been on the Sandown – Newport Road and went in chimney first. Unfortunately the fitters had chocked and packed the front end of the locomotive. As the engine moved forward there was a terrible crunching sound as the chimney made contact with the brickwork. I had a good laugh that day.

Eddie Spears

I started on the Island railways in March 1950, but had come down to the Isle of Wight from my home in Northumberland as a soldier during the War. We were based at Blackwater, and used to watch the two coach trains pass by to Merstone and Sandown. I laughed at these cute little trains, but never thought that I would end up working on them after the War.

For many years I was a relief signalman which meant I had to travel all over the Island to look after the different boxes where signalmen were off duty on holiday or sick. During the summer service, I used to go to Smallbrook Junction with my opposite numbers Vic Hailes and Ray Draper. This was probably the most photographed signalbox even by normal standards, and unusual in that it had a knee frame with the interlocking contained inside

Station Foreman Les Allen supervises the shunting at Ryde St. John's Road on 8 June 1965. The engine at the other end is No. 14 *Fishbourne*.

John Goss

Engine No. 21 *Sandown*, driven by Eddie Prangnell, approaches Smallbrook Road Bridge with a train for Ventnor, during the period of time each year when the sections between St. John's Road and Brading, on the Ventnor Line, and St. John's Road and Haven Street, were operated as two parallel lines. Note the sleeper built fogman's hut on the right of the picture.

Dr Gerald R. Siviour

With the points clipped and the signal arms removed for the winter, No. 26 *Whitwell* makes her way towards Smallbrook with a train for Newport and Cowes.

Dr Gerald R. Siviour

On board a down Ventnor train, waiting at Smallbrook Junction inner home signal, as an up Ventnor train crosses from the single to double line to clear the section.

John Goss

Signalman Vic Hailes has just collected the single line token from the fireman of No. 33 *Bembridge* with a train from Ventnor. Smooth working of Smallbrook Junction governed the operation of the entire system. A signal check of no more than a minute or so could soon react right through to Ventnor and Cowes and back again due to the tight crossing schedules at the passing stations further down the line.

R. E. Burroughs

Perfect timing for an action picture. Signalman Vic Hailes gives the token to the fireman of the 2.55p.m. Ryde Pier Head – Sandown train at Smallbrook Junction on 14 June 1958.

H. Peter Mason

Summer at Smallbrook Junction in 1929. Three years earlier this signalbox was opened for the first time — not completely built and minus a roof.

George H. Hunt

At an approach speed of 30m.p.h. Signalman Eddie Spears prepares to collect the token from the driver of a train from Ventnor on 31 July 1965.

Anthony E. Bennett

a casing above floor level. On summer Saturdays I think it was the busiest box controlling single lines on British Railways, with ten trains an hour — one every six minutes. Sometimes if a Ventnor train was late from Brading we would have to hold one or two trains. This could react right through to Ventnor, and back again with the tight crossing schedules at the passing stations further down the line — the name of Eddie Spears would then be mud!

Smallbrook was situated at the junction of the Cowes and Ventnor lines, but my job working the box only ran between May and September. During the winter time-table I had to go back to work at Ryde Pier as the double track was worked as two independent lines. After electrification in 1967, and the closure of the Cowes Line, Smallbrook was no longer required. It so happened that I was the last signalman to take the token on 17 September 1966 from the fireman of engine No. 35 *Freshwater*.

The twenty-lever box at Smallbrook used to be open from 3.45 in the morning until 11.30 at night, but after about 5 in the afternoon the timetable used to be less hectic. Besides operating the levers our job was to pass the token to the fireman. This was a large leather hoop with a pouch containing an aluminium key. On odd occasions the fireman would drop the token and it would bounce. I have seen one fall under the wheels of the engine and been sliced in half. The key token used to govern the starting signals and points so that only one train could enter the single line at a time. During the summer I used the pouch to pass on cricket results, which I had heard on my illegal radio, to the footplate crews.

At Wroxall we operated another system using a brass staff. This would occasionally be hot when received from the passing firemen who used to heat it up for a joke. Other times I would have the joke on them. Let me journey back in time to Smallbrook days . . . it was getting on towards teatime and the cricket scores were coming through on my illegal radio in the signalbox. A goods train left Haven Street for Ryde, and that was the last I remember of it. Meanwhile a train went through from Brading, and a train went on to Brading. The telephone rang from Haven Street, and asked if the goods train had gone through to Ryde. I genuinely thought that the train had gone. Eventually the inspector from Ryde telephoned, 'We are beginning to go up the wall. Pull your distant signal from Cowes.' Presently I heard a whistle. It was my fault of course, but it was funny to keep Jim Hunnybun waiting. What had happened was that Jim who was the driver sent Percy Primmer the guard up to the box. Percy had seen me running from side to side on the telephone, and thought everything was in hand. I had assumed that they had gone past and thought no more about them.

There was a lot of nice wild life out at Smallbrook. A pheasant strode along towards the box one night from the Cowes Road. By chance a lengthsman had left his shotgun in the box ready loaded. That's my dinner, I thought! I crept around the Ventnor side of the box and stalked up on her. I looked at the bird and hesitated, as it was just not me to kill something so beautiful. Suddenly, the bird flew off, the shotgun went off in the air and missed it completely.

That was not my worst mistake. My first day at work at Newport was one to remember! I was asked to do some shunting as I had worked down the mines in the North East and I knew a little about shunting wagons. The idea at Newport was to sort out the empty wagons from the full ones before the tradesmen arrived later in the morning. My job was to pull the points and send the empties towards the right hand siding, and the full towards the left. The foreman kept shouting at me to pull the points. Just as some empties were crossing over he shouted again and so I obeyed as instructed. Well, one half the wagon went one way and the other half in the opposite direction. When the foreman arrived on the scene to tell me off I replied, 'Well, Sir, I did as you said!'

Ray Draper

My Island railway career began at the Office of the Assistant for the Isle of Wight, Ryde St. John's Road Station. The Assistant in those days was Mr H.D. Tahourdin, and this is what he said about me in a character reference:

To whom it may concern.

This is to certify that Raymond Draper has been employed at these Works as an Office lad since 4th June, 1925, and I have pleasure in stating that I have found him to be a very useful, willing and industrious lad. He is a good time-keeper, and I think he will make good in any position to which he may be appointed.

When I left the Works at Ryde old Bill Smith organised a collection for me amongst the staff. They presented me with a silver pocket watch, suitably inscribed.

From St. John's Road, I moved two stations down the line to Sandown where Mr Alec Wheway was stationmaster. Now every Christmas, a local firm, Chapmans, used to give a turkey to the stationmaster. During a game of football amongst all the porters, clerks and station staff at Sandown, the Christmas turkey was delivered. Fred Fowler, the booking clerk boiled over with rage at the sight of the stationmaster's free Christmas dinner. 'I'll be blowed. We do all the work and he gets the turkey,' Fred said. With that he jumped on the bird until it was as flat as a pancake. When Mr Wheway arrived to collect his turkey, Fred told him, 'We do the work, you get the reward!' The stationmaster retrieved the remains of the bird and walked away without saying a word. Some time later he returned and had this to say to Fred Fowler, 'I've told my wife what you said about that turkey. My wife told me to tell you — the Lord knows where poverty lies.'

I remember about the same time Alec Wheway and the Divisional Superintendent went down to Alverstone to examine the station accounts which were in a mess. Now Alverstone came under the jurisdiction of Mr Wheway as Sandown stationmaster. When Alec returned he told us all, 'What do you think the Divisional Superintendent said? . . . It wasn't anything wrong with the accounts; it was lack of supervision.'

At the age of twenty, in 1930, I moved to Mill Hill on

Soon after midnight on 17/18 September 1966 at Small-brook Junction Signalbox, preparations are made to remove the single line token instruments and board up the windows before locking the door. This was an annual procedure, since Smallbrook was normally closed for the winter. With the closure of the Newport – Cowes Line and the Shanklin electrification, the box was no longer required as the remaining pointwork was controlled from Ryde St. John's Road Signalbox.

Tim R. Genower

A sad occasion for Signalman Eddie Spears at Small-brook Junction, as he takes the token from the driver of No. 35 *Freshwater* on the final train of the day. After this the box was closed for the last time on 17 September 1966.

Tim R. Genower

Removing essential signalling/token instruments for transfer to Ryde St. John's Road Signalbox.

Tim R. Genower

The Smallbrook Junction Signalbox token instrument.
Dr John Mackett

Signalman Ray Draper pulls the levers inside Smallbrook Box to allow a train from Brading to Smallbrook along the single line through Whitefield Woods on 5 September 1957. *H. Peter Mason*

Approximately five minutes after Signalman Draper accepted the 9.40a.m. Ventnor – Ryde Pier Head train, he collects the token outside the box. *H. Peter Mason*

the outskirts of Cowes. I remained here for ten years as a grade one porter, and can well remember queues of passengers fifteen yards long waiting for tickets — a very regular occurrence in those days. Otto Hill was the stationmaster of Mill Hill, and he would shout, 'Don't forget to switch the lights off,' before leaving work every night.

My opposite number was a very interesting character, Arthur Dark. Each Thursday the early and late turn porters would clean the floor of the station waiting room. If Arthur was on the early turn, he would draw a chalk line down the centre of the room. 'I have cleaned this half. That's yours,' he would say. My half of the room to be cleaned would be that including the fireplace!

During the early part of the last War, I transferred to Newport as a signalman. It was the night signalman's duty to walk down to the South Box and open the Medina drawbridge. As I made my way down to do this job one night, I heard the sound of laughter and merriment coming from the Locomotive Sheds. After opening the drawbridge, I wandered over to see what all the noise was about and looked through the window. The cleaners, fireman, drivers and shed staff were all assembled around a table. In their midst, dancing on the table, was a naked woman who originated from Cowes!

When I was working at the North Box one day, there was a lot of trouble at South Box. Apparently, they required an oil stove at Pan Lane Crossing and the stationmaster at Newport, Alec Wheway, walked down to the South Box and asked Signalman Harold Blundey for his oil stove. Harold was wise to what was happening and placed a chain around the stove and a pipe and placed a padlock on it. Presently Mr Wheway sent a porter down to South Box to collect the stove, who reported back to the stationmaster that the stove was locked and chained. As soon as Alec Wheway heard this news, he walked down to South Box and asked Signalman Blundey for the stove. 'Help yourself,' replied Harold Blundey. 'How the hell can I, It's chained?' said Mr Wheway. They returned to the station and summoned Ern Landon the Inspector, to retrieve the stove from South Box. Again they had no success in acquiring the stove. Finally Mr G.H. Gardiner the Assistant for the Isle of Wight Railways walked down to South Box. 'Now what is this all about, Harold? You are to hand over that stove now,' demanded Mr. Gardiner. 'Help yourself,' replied Harold, and he bent down to the lock and just flicked it over with his fingers. All that time the lock was open!

From 1957, I went on to the relief signalling staff on the Island, joining Eddie Spears and Vic Hailes out at

'The Golden Mile.' Due to an earth slip between Brading and Sandown, single line working was introduced on the up line of the double track section. This required very stringent safety precautions, and either Ray Draper or Eddie Spears would act as pilotman, carrying a wrong line ticket on the footplate of the engine and keeping a sharp look out on the wrong line. Ray Draper, acting as pilotman, is on the footplate of No. 35 *Freshwater* leaving Brading with a down train on 12 March 1966.

Timothy P. Cooper

SOUTHERN RAILWAY.

R. E. L. MAUNSELL,
Chief Mechanical Engineer,
WATERLOO, S.E. 1.

H. D. TAHOURDIN.
ASSISTANT FOR
ISLE OF WIGHT, RYDE,
ST. JOHN'S ROAD, I.O.W.

OFFICE OF ASSISTANT FOR ISLE OF WIGHT,

RYDE (ST. JOHN'S ROAD STATION),

ISLE OF WIGHT.

30th January, 1926.

PLEASE REFER TO

IN YOUR REPLY.

TO WHOM IT MAY CONCERN.

        This is to certify that RAYMOND RAY DRAPER
has been employed at these works as a Office Lad since
4th June, 1925, and I have pleasure in stating that I have
found him to be a very useful, willing and industrious lad.
He is a good-time-keeper, and I think he will make good in
any position to which he may be appointed.

H. D. Tahourdin

A valuable piece of paper in 1926!

A perfect token exchange at Smallbrook Junction
between Signalman Ray Draper and the driver of '02'
No. 20 *Shanklin* on 28 May 1966.

John Goss

Smallbrook Junction during the summer season. Quite often I was called on to do pilot working. Here is an example; there was an earth slip near Sandown in the winter of 1965/66, and we had to go over to single line working. This required very stringent safety precautions to be strictly observed. As pilotman, I had to wear an official armband, and would have to give the driver of a train a 'Wrong Line Ticket' which would be handed personally to the signalman at the end of the single line section. Of course I would have to travel up on the footplate to keep a look out. The drivers nicknamed the stretch of track between Brading and Sandown, 'Ray Draper's Golden Mile'. I may have earned some money as pilotman, but I earned it the hard way at all hours of the day, seven days a week, in all weather!

I remember working for a time at Ryde Pier Head Box and being amazed at the arrival of the horse boat. A tug used to haul two flat barges across the Spithead into Ryde on the high tide. The tug would bring the barges in as close as possible to the Esplanade, where the Hovercraft Terminal is now. We would then release them and with the aid of long punting poles they would bring them in further. The barge sides would then be dropped and the animals — horses, cattle, sheep and pigs — would swim ashore the remaining short distance. This unusual service was provided originally by the Southern Railway and latterly by British Railways Southern Region. The paddle steamer boat service with *Ryde, Whippingham* and *Sandown*, between Portsmouth and Ryde Pier Head, was also operated by the Railways. I remember watching the biggest paddle steamer, the *Whippingham*, trying to tie up one day during rough seas. First they would get the bow tied up but not the stern, then let go and come in from a different angle, with little success again. A little cockney shouted, 'Hold on there, Captain, we'll bring the Pier out to you.' We had a good working relationship with the lads on the boats in those days, as I found out when I finished my career as a Pier Head Inspector.

Roy Way

My railway career which spanned over half a century started in Ryde St. John's Road Works as a boy labourer in February 1924. My first job was to strip the upholstery from the old Freshwater and Yarmouth carriage stock for retrimming by two coach trimmers Albert Fasbrook and Hector Holbrook. Mr Fasbrook was a first class workman, having worked on the Egyptian State coaches at the Birmingham Carriage and Wagon Works at Smethwick. He was working at Newport Carriage Works one day when a bird flew in to the shop, picked up one of his needles and flew off with it. I remember Albert chasing after it shouting, 'Whoa! Whoa!' with little effect.

'Pheasant Alley' in winter. Engine No. 32 *Bonchurch* steams through Whitefield Woods with a six coach Ventnor train, picking up speed down the falling gradient. Footplate crews were often retrieving pheasants for their dinners along this stretch of line — hence it became known as 'Pheasant Alley'.

Dr Gerald R. Siviour

With an approach speed of between 40 and 50m.p.h., No. 33 *Bembridge* passes under Truckell's Bridge with the 1.20p.m. to Shanklin on 20 June 1964.

John Goss

Some five miles from Ryde Pier Head, a down train to Ventnor, (headed by an unidentified '02') enters Brading Station sometime in 1933. Note the weighing machines under the awning on the up platform.

George H. Hunt

Brading, 1930, by Jimmy James

Signalman Jess Wheeler walks to the platform edge at Brading Station ready to collect the token from Fireman Charlie Hackett on No. 35 *Freshwater*.

Mike Esau

Signalman Jess Wheeler prepares to collect the single line token from the fireman of the 12.25p.m. Ryde Pier Head – Ventnor train as it arrives at Brading on a cold, snowy 1 January 1963.

H. Peter Mason

The Isle of Wight Railway Company had amongst its variety of coaching stock several 'three compartment stock'; comprising a small Third compartment at each end with a wide First Class compartment in the middle which had the usual long seats, and a double backed armchair in the middle. On Ashey Race Meeting days these coaches were made up together and Mr Holbrook removed the double backed chairs and replaced them with tables. The train was then taken up the railway line which ran up to the chalk pit, and was put behind the Grandstand and used as a Restaurant Train during the Race Meeting. During Ashey Race days we had several travelling Ticket Collectors from the mainland, and Race Specials used to run into the down loop line at Ryde St. John's Road, and all the tickets collected here by them were sorted and tied up by myself and colleagues who were on duty at the time.

My signalling career on the Island Railways started at Newchurch in January 1931 as a grade one porter signalman. During my time at Newchurch I had an old gentleman ask for the following ticket, 'I don't want a return. I wants one to go and one to come and miss a train or two.' Also an American who was working at a new bore hole at Niton Water Works at the time, asked for 'a round trip to Newport.' This was the station from which one of the earliest broadcasts of carol singing took place. The carol singers would sing in Dick Whittington's booking office, hence the sound would be relayed via the telephone circuit to Horringford and stations on the Sandown – Newport line.

Newchurch was an 'Intermediate Block Post' and level crossing signalbox. It had two Preece's, one wire Block instrument, and a 'push and switch' for long and short working between Sandown and Merstone. This was only in use when I was on duty as my relief was a junior porter.

One day I had a telephone call from the next station down the line at Horringford to say that a parcel was on its way down the line from him. What happened was that from a previous train he had a goat deposited on him for collection. My colleague Syd Dennett at Horringford had tethered the animal to the platform fence, but unfortunately the next train scared the goat who broke loose and high tailed it down to Newchurch. As he walked down towards me I walked towards him, and finally we captured it. I didn't envy him his journey back to Horringford!

Rolland Gallop, signalman at Sandown Box has now passed on. I worked with Roll for quite some time and he was a jolly good signalman and friend — we never had a harsh word. Roll was late for work and was visited by the late Mr de Pury who was the Assistant Divisional Superintendent for the Isle of Wight at the time. The conversation went something like this. 'Well Gallop, what made you late for work?' 'Well, it's like this, sir: my wife and I are passionately fond of pickled onions, so for supper we opened a jar and ate the lot. Consequence was I overslept.' Mr. de Pury replied, 'Damned good, Gallop — that will do this time, but next time don't bring your wife into it or else it will have to go to Waterloo.'

Sandown to Merstone was worked by 'Train Staff and Ticket'. The tickets were kept in a box and were released by a key on the end of the staff. This system was devised so that if you had two trains going to Merstone before one was returning from Merstone to Sandown the first train would travel on a ticket which was given to the driver of that train and the driver of the next train would carry the staff.

On Sundays the last train from Merstone always carried the ticket. As the Monday was a Bank Holiday in the case to follow, the first train from Sandown should have carried the staff to Merstone. The signalman at Merstone on this occasion sent the train on a ticket, but shortly afterwards realised his mistake. He contacted the signalman at Merstone and informed him of his error, and told him he would take the staff by road to Wroxall on the Ventnor Line and send it down to him from there. The powers that be were thus none the wiser, which was a good thing as there would have been a lot of explaining to do, with the Rules and Regulations being broken willy nilly.

Some of my happiest days were spent at Brading signalbox. Here the signalman controlled the double track to Sandown, and the junction for the short branch to St. Helen's and Bembridge. The branch trains were accommodated in a bay road on the eastern side of the down platform. The layout was such that an engine could run round its train without interfering with the main Ryde – Ventnor lines. In its heyday there was a small goods yard at the Ryde end of the station and a long chalk siding running parallel with the main line at the Ventnor end of the station. The Bembridge Branch was opened on 27 May 1882. The train was known as 'Grattie Winkle' by the locals at Bembridge, St. Helen's and Brading. The engine was shipped to Malta during the 1914-18 War and never returned.

On one of the window panes in Brading Box is the name of J. Lacy, who was one of the early signalmen, and he had written his name with a diamond. He used to mend watches and clocks, so I was told by one of his relations; also I discovered parts of watches and clocks in his locker. This was not the only work carried out in Brading Box besides signalling. One signalman used to repair his children's shoes during his period of duty.

This is the story of two ladies, wives of a signalman and guard from Brading. Kept in the Booking Office at Brading was a Market Pass for use between Brading and Ryde Esplanade for the use of the staff on Tuesdays. Thus on this day one could look out of the Box windows and witness a race between the two ladies, one coming down the station road, the other across the field — both red in the face in a race to get the pass. It got so bad that they had to call a truce and share it out alternately.

There were two guards who worked the Bembridge Branch, Walter Buckett and Alfred Dallimore (Bewley and Dally), both characters, yet very different. Bewley came up to me one day fuming. Apparently some passenger had asked him if Dally was his brother. 'Do I look like him, I ask you. No, nothing like him — fellow must be a damned fool!' Bewley worked a train from Bembridge and on arrival at Brading the train was empty, but when he took his tail lamp off to place it at the rear end of the train for the return to Bembridge, he still called out 'All change. All Change. Over the bridge for Ryde.' Bewley was always on the look out for a tip from the passengers and this is a story related to me by one of the branch drivers. Bewley had taken a package for a lady of note at Bembridge, and at times they had quite a time to spare before they left for Brading. Bewley said to this driver just before they were due to depart, 'If only I had a light I would have taken the package up to her and she would have given me something.' To which the driver replied, 'Well, you had your headlamp.' 'Damn my buttons,' said Bewley, 'so I have; why didn't I think of that!'

During the last War Bewley was involved in a tragedy at Brading in which a soldier stationed at Culver Fort was shot, and subsequently died of his wounds. Walter had worked the train from Bembridge, and on arrival at Brading a young soldier alighted from the train and crossed the line and hid himself in a dark corner on the up platform to Ryde. Then two armed soldiers appeared on the down platform and started to search the branch train. When Walter was taking his tail lamp back, he asked them what they were looking for and they told him. He pointed to the poor unfortunate soldier who immediately made a run for it and was shot. The result was an Official Enquiry by the civil police and the military in which Walter was summoned to attend. He was required to give evidence at Culver twice and later Winchester, and it was on his evidence that the Corporal who did the shooting was not discharged from the Army.

Dally was always playing pranks on Bewley. One Christmas Eve, Dally placed two new half crowns on the shelf just above the steam heater in the guard's van, and he timed it just as Bewley was stepping into the van to take over. Dally would sweep the two coins up in his hands saying, 'Damn me if I didn't forget to pick up those two half crowns Lord so and so gave me at Bembridge,' and so off home. Bewley as soon as he arrived at Bembridge went straight into Charlie Wetherick in the Booking Office and asked Charlie if he saw Lord so and so give Dally the coins 'No,' said Charlie, 'he got them from me.' 'There's a bad fellow for you who does it on purpose.'

Dally was a keen gardener and he was always saying how big everything was that he grew, like 'rasberries four to the pound', 'pumpkins as big as an air raid shelter.' He was quite a scrounger when the local farmers used to bring their milk to send to Portsmouth by train, always asking them if they had any seed spuds left? The farmer would ask how many he required, at which he would ask for enough to finish out a row or two.

Driver Charlie Humphries was the driver of the first train from Bembridge one morning, and after uncoupling the engine was down at the water column when the down train from Ryde drew in with Driver Jack Sturgess smiling out of the cab of his engine No. 22 *Brading* as he entered. Charlie shouted to Jack, 'I don't want anymore to do with you main line drivers if you can't keep time.' Throughout the rest of the week it was so still that you could hear Mad Jack start up from Ryde St. John's

Road, full out all the way. He would be standing in the station at Brading as Charlie (nicknamed 'Klinker') would be just running into St. Helen's Station with the branch train. That is something I shall never forget.

One severe winter, Jack was the driver on the branch train, he had done several trips and when trying to take water the outlet valves were found to be frozen. Mr Marten the stationmaster came to me and said that Jack would have to throw the fire out if he could not get water as his tanks were empty. The ice on top of the water column was nearly an inch thick, so I climbed up the ladder and broke the ice with the engine coal pricker. Gradually I managed to free the outlet valve from inside the tank and saved the day, but had two weeks at home with flu for my pains.

On one memorable occasion Len Creath was having some trouble with the little Peters two stroke engine which drove the water pump for pumping the water up into the water tanks for branch engines and main line locomotives which wished to top up. He stripped the engine right down and reassembled it, but he could not get the machine to go. I saw this all going on from the signalbox, and had some time to pass so looked into the shed where Len said he had tried everything known to science, and was about to strip it down again. I said to Len, 'Have you filled the tank with paraffin?' He replied that he had, so I suggested that he try something not known to science. We disconnected the paraffin and put some petrol in and the engine started. Len quickly reconnected the paraffin and all was well, as I found out when I had to work the engine pump.

I had some fun and games with engine and pump. One day the pump would not work so I had the stationmaster with me and we took the top off and poured water into it with the engine running to prime the pump. On this occasion the stationmaster was looking down to see if the pump was starting to pick up the water when all of a sudden it did and shot water into his face, knocking his hat off and soaking his smart dark uniform. He took it all in good humour though.

At Brading the branch engine during the morning used to leave the train in the branch platform then used to go to St. Helen's to shunt the Quay. During this time we used to wash the train down with water from the station fire buckets, using a wartime stirrup pump to squirt the water. The fire buckets were spaced so far apart and our stationmaster, Mr N. Attrill, was working the pump and walking backwards towards the next bucket. He was concentrating so much on directing the water in the right place that as he retreated down the platform backwards he promptly sat down in a full bucket, much to my enjoyment in the signalbox. He saw the funny side of it.

One day at Brading Box I recall we were having points and signal connections renewed. This job was undertaken by the local S. & T. (Signal and Telegraph) fitters along with some from the mainland. The task entailed the disconnection of the points for the Bembridge Branch run-round. The levers involved were numbers 8, 9 ground signals and 10 and 14 points. It was agreed between the S. & T. men and myself that they would leave one end of 14 points and disconnect the end nearest

A signalman's eye view of No. 16 *Ventnor* at Brading on 30 December 1966 — the penultimate day of Isle of Wight steam — with the 12.30p.m. ex-Ryde.

John Goss

Bembridge, and plug and clip it for the branch train into the station. After the passing of the train they would unplug and clip, reverse the points for the engine to run round and back on to the train. However, unfortunately they forgot to do it, so that when I set up my end the engine ran through their end of 14 points and split them. Luckily the engine did not become derailed, and there was a loud cry from the mainland fitters for our fitter to come to the rescue. To add to the troubles the Assistant for the Isle of Wight came off the down train from Ryde and walked up into the box to enquire what was the matter, so I had to do a bit of quick thinking and said, 'They don't fit very well, sir, but will be all right very soon and there will be no delay to the branch train.'

Also the Permanent Way inspector came off the down train, and he went out to have a look at things and asked the fitter if he had signed the Train Register, which he had not. The Inspector let it go and told the fitter not to let it happen again.

Alexander Wheway

I was over fifty years on the Island railways and retired from Newport in 1949. My career began on the Isle of Wight Railway Company line, and started off at Ventnor as a booking clerk. From there I moved to Wroxall just after the Southern took over, in about 1923,

where I was stationmaster, and gradually through the years I gained promotion to Sandown and eventually the 'plum job' at Newport in 1940.

My family moved from Nuneaton in Warwickshire, and we lived at Brading. My father was connected with the railways in that he took passengers from the Isle of Wight Railway line to St. Lawrence or Appuldurcombe House by horse and trap, so, you see, railways were in my blood to begin with. But for working on the railway I would not have met my wife. She lived at Shanklin and used to travel to work by train. We met on the platform at Sandown and it was love at first sight.

We had some colourful characters on the Island railways in those days. Take old Bert Pullinger, the station foreman at Newport. I used to watch him for hours. It was a trick of his to tell young drivers and firemen to wait outside his office, and then address someone inside, telling them not to let any one in until he returned. He could then leave his office unlocked and safe — but of course there was no one inside it; he just made everyone believe someone was looking after things! You had to watch the staff very carefully, but provided they did their work a little horseplay didn't matter.

An early morning smoke screen at Brading from No. 28 *Ashey* leaving on the 6.46a.m. to Ventnor on 9 July 1965.

John Goss

Sandown Station by Jimmy James

Sandown Station staff in 1929

		George H. Hunt
Fred Fowler (Booking Clerk)	Rolland Gallop (Signalman)	Fred Squibb (Booking Clerk)
Ted Harley (Porter/Signalman)	Alec Wheway (Station Master)	John Willcocks (Grade 2 Porter)
	Reg Seaman	Raymond Draper

A friendly atmosphere prevailed on the Island railways for many years after Grouping, most particularly on the old Isle of Wight Railway, probably because there were often several people from one family on the railway; the three Vallender brothers, two of whom were enginemen, and another engineman family were the Toogoods. Indeed I had three brothers on the railways — two clerks and one porter signalman. Perhaps another reason for the family atmosphere was that the last General Manager of the Isle of Wight Railway, Mr H. K. Day, who was a Brading man, recruited to the railway many of the boys from Brading School.

The junior porter at Newchurch was a young lad by the name of Arthur Tosdevin. Once, I remember, I had been ringing Newchurch on the telephone for over half an hour without any reply. Eventually I did manage to get through and the conversation went as follows: 'Tosdevin, where have you been?' The young junior porter replied, 'I had a bite on the end of my fishing line and couldn't leave it, Sir.' On another occasion I decided to stroll down the line from Sandown, where I was stationmaster, around the curve through Alverstone to Newchurch. It was astonishing to discover young Tosdevin sitting on the crossing gates with a girl on either side of him!

One morning I was on duty at Sandown on the up platform, when two elderly ladies came up to me and asked 'Which way to Shanklin please?' I replied, 'Through the subway and follow the other passengers.' They did, right up into Sandown High Street! Needless to say they had quite a bit to say to me on their return; the mentality of some people is amazing.

Copy.

ISLE OF WIGHT   CENTRAL RAILWAY.

Manager's Office.

Newport I.W.

9th February 1888

Notice to Staff Generally.

Note that on Saturday 11th inst., Special Royal Trains will run as under and the undermentioned instructions must be rigidly adhered to, in order the exact times of running may be kept.

		A.	B.
Ryde St. Johns Rd.	dep:	1.50pm.	4.50pm.
Whippingham.	arr:	2.0 pm.	5.0 pm.

Whippingham	dep:	2.45pm.
Ryde St. Johns Rd.	arr:	2.54pm.

A.   Will take Ticket Ashey to Whippingham and shunt there to allow 2.18pm Ryde to Newport to pass.   This train must not be signalled on Electric Block between Wootton and Newport.

B.   Will run on to Newport after setting down passengers at Whippingham, and return empty to Ryde during the evening.

The following trains must run punctually to time, and no wagons attached under any circumstances, and all parties will be held responsible to see same is carried out.   The 1.15 Newport to Ryde; the 2.18pm Ryde to Newport to run from Haven Street to Wootton two minutes in advance of time shewn on bills and keep a good look-out for signals at Whippingham. The 4.15pm Newport to Ryde not to wait for Sandown train at Newport if not to time;   the 3.35pm Ryde to Newport to start to time.   Engine to work these Special Trains will leave Newport for Ryde at 12.55pm.   Newport Ashey and Ryde St. Johns Rd Stations, to see that proper Train Staff and Tickets are given to respective trains so as not to be thrown out of correct working.   The 1.50pm Ryde to Whippingham to take Train Ticket. the 4.50pm Ryde to Whippingham to take Ticket Ryde to Ashey and Staff Ashey to Newport.   The 2.45pm Whippingham to Ryde will be piloted by the undersigned between Whippingham and Ashey, and take Train Staff Ticket Ashey to Ryde.

Ashey to have Train Staff and Tickets in readiness on Platform to hand enginemen when running through.

H. Simmonds
Manager.

One of the saddest days of my life was when they closed the Sandown – Newport Line in February 1956. The last trains were the 07.50p.m. from Sandown, which arrived at Newport at 8.16p.m., and the 7.49p.m. from Newport arriving at Sandown at 8.20p.m., crossing at Merstone Junction. Normally, for the last trains of the night on this line there would be only a few dozen passengers. For these trains, however, they could not pack them on enough.

Engine No. 17 *Seaview*, crewed by Bill Vallender driving and D. Owers firing, took their train with guard Bill Dibden aboard out of Newport and across the Medina Drawbridge for the last time to Sandown. Dozens of detonators exploded, echoing across Newport. In the opposite direction, Jack Nicholson drove engine No. 33 *Bembridge* out of Sandown; on a wreath of laurels was inscribed, 'In loving memory of a good and faithful servant. Born 1 February 1875, passed away 5 February 1956.' The ITV were there to film this sad occasion at Sandown and they caught up with us again at Merstone to capture the two trains passing. It's a great pity the public didn't support the trains more before that final night. If they had travelled on them more, they would still be with us today. It was particularly bitter for me as I had been the stationmaster at Sandown and Newport and now many of my old friends who had worked on the line had to move away to other jobs.

The Isle of Wight has long had a tradition of being a holiday home for the Royal Family. This tradition has its origins in the reign of Queen Victoria and her Island residence at Osbourne House near East Cowes. Queen Victoria originally had Whippingham Station opened as her exclusive private station for the Royal residence at Osbourne. Later the station was opened to the public, although I recall that many Royal visitors and dignitaries continued to use it, to a lesser extent.

The Royals used the Island railways quite frequently until World War II. Of course, when they travelled by train on official occasions a Royal Train had to be commissioned. For instance, a special Royal Train was marshalled up by the Isle of Wight Central Railway in order to convey Queen Victoria from Whippingham to Ventnor via Ryde St. John's Road for the opening of the National Consumptive Hospital in February 1888. This was a very colourful event on the Island Railways, and everything had to be ship shape and Bristol fashion with trains running punctually. After Queen Victoria died, the Royals rarely frequented Osbourne House. However, they did visit the Isle of Wight for Cowes Week and on special occasions like the Naval Reviews. During their visits to the Island the Royal Family would quite often travel incognito into Newport or Ryde by the normal service train. Occasionally railway staff would recognise the distinguished passengers and tip off other staff at stations down the line. One particular story comes to mind concerning the two small Royal Princesses, some time before World War II. The driver of the Cowes to Newport train spotted two small figures with a tall lady on the platform of Cowes Station, as he puffed away out of the platform towards Newport. Now the lady hailed the departing train to stop, and naturally, as was the Island railway custom, he halted his train and reversed back. He collected his grateful passengers and continued on his short journey to Newport, thinking little more about this everyday occurrence. Upon arrival at Newport the stationmaster greeted the three passengers, 'bowing and scraping' all the way. Now the driver, whose name was 'Bonnie' Baines, and guard Harry Groves, later discovered from me at Sandown who their passengers were. I had received a telephone message from Newport informing me that the passengers on the train were no less than Princess Elizabeth (later to become Queen

Sandown Station in 1929. Six years earlier the station buildings on the down platform had been the headquarters of the Isle of Wight Railway Company. A subway connected the up main and bay platforms to the down platform. Note the signal box which is located above the up side platform, giving the signalman an excellent view of the station approaches.

George H. Hunt

Elizabeth) and Princess Margaret.

A close relative of mine was the stationmaster at Brading for some considerable time. On one particular occasion he was on the platform at Brading when a passenger alighted from a train and approached him with an enquiry. 'Not now, not now please. I've got three trains in the station at the moment and things are very hectic.' It was true there were the Ryde – Ventnor, Ventnor – Ryde Pier Head trains passing, and the Bembridge Branch train waiting in the bay platform. After the trains had all departed my stationmaster relative apologised to the passenger. 'That's all right, I fully understand. I'm stationmaster at Waterloo,' replied the passenger.

During the happy period of time that I was stationmaster at Sandown, I was required to preside over a very amusing complaint from a passenger. Apparently he was travelling home to Ryde, and owing to his corpulent frame he had encountered some difficulty in boarding the train. The Island-born booking clerk observed the portly passenger struggling to get through the carriage door. Using his initiative he said to the passenger 'Ere — you had better go by goods train.' This comment incensed the passenger who complained to me. I had to reprimand the booking clerk at the time, but when I look back now I can laugh at the incident.

Len Sheath

I was the last serving railwayman who was with the old Isle of Wight Railway Company. As a boy aged 15½ I left Sandown Secondary School to join the railway as a messenger boy in the office at Sandown. That was in 1922 and only ten months later the Railways Reorganisation Act meant the takeover of the Island company by the old London and South Western, in the form of the Southern Railway. I recall working with Alec Wheway, who presided at Sandown as stationmaster, Bert Harley, who was in charge of the parcels office, and Fred Fowler and Fred Squibb who were the booking clerks. Eventually I was promoted from top grade porter to signalbox duties. It was Haven Street signalbox that I first worked in, which of course is now happily fully restored to working order by the Wight Locomotive Society. It was here we had a hammock in the box to sleep in.

Later came World War II, when I had to cycle to Merstone to man the signalbox at that busy junction of the Sandown – Newport and Ventnor West Branch lines. Here the agricultural community provided plenty of business for the railway, with as many as three trains a day leaving Merstone, fully loaded with locally grown sugar beet. This beet was then shipped over to the mainland from Medina Wharf for processing. The highlight of

The Isle of Wight Railway Company General Manager's office staff, pictured on Sandown Station platform in 1922.
Back row: Len Sheath, Bill Hendridge, Reg Sheath, Eddie Taylor
Middle row: Topsy Evans, John Bull, Inspector Malcolm Buckett, Jim Butcher, Dorothy Perkins, Sam Prismall
Front row: Willie Wood, Mr. Pidgeon, H. K. Day (General Manager), Mickey Newman, Mr. Shaw, Fred Perkin (Company Auditor)
Len Sheath Collection

Signalman Len Sheath with the Sandown – Merstone single line staff at Sandown Station in 1948.

Len Sheath Collection

Driver Frank Ash on No. 32 *Bonchurch* collects the token from Signalman Len Sheath at Sandown Station, on 7 August 1964.

Peter J. Relf

A period picture of an Isle of Wight Railway 2-4-0 Beyer Peacock departing from Sandown. Note the collection of four wheel coaches and the polished copper capped chimney.

Timothy P. Cooper Collection

Sandown Station as Driver Gerald Coombes on No. 21 *Sandown* prepares to climb away up the 1:80 gradient past Los Altos Park towards Shanklin and Ventnor.

Dr Gerald R. Siviour

'The Tourist' through train leaves Sandown for Ventnor behind Drummond boilered No. 27 *Merstone*, on 18 August 1934. This was the first summer that 'The Tourist' through train could be hauled all the way by an '02'. This was due to strengthening of the bridges on the Freshwater Line. The timetable for this train was now accelerated, leaving Ventnor at 9.55a.m., calling at Wroxall, Shanklin, Sandown, Newport, Yarmouth and arriving at Freshwater at 11.12a.m. It would return from Freshwater at 5.20p.m. and arrive back at Ventnor by 6.46p.m. in time for the holidaymakers' hotel dinner.
C. G. Woodnutt/Timothy P. Cooper Collection

A hectic time at Shanklin. No. 20 *Shanklin* prepares to depart for Sandown and Ryde, whilst No. 14 *Fishbourne* enters the station. Recognisable in the picture are Signalman Len Langbourne, Fireman Charlie Hackett and George Mears.
Dr Gerald R. Siviour

Shanklin Station in 1929, approximately 8½ miles from Ryde Pier Head. Pictured are the up and down platforms, and the small goods yard close to the down platform. The signalbox roof is just visible above the up platform canopy and was elevated above the up platform. Shanklin was the terminus of the Isle of Wight Railway from 1864 to 1866, and has been the end of the line for the remaining electrified section since 1966.
George H. Hunt

Shanklin Station by Jimmy James

Wroxall Station in 1930, which served the large village, had a passing loop installed by the Southern Railway in 1925. it was always an attractive station, decked with flowers on the platforms. Trains would halt here for several minutes for an oil lamp to be placed in each compartment for the run through the tunnel to Ventnor, prior to electric carriage lighting. Note the elevated ramp on the up platform for loading and unloading parcels from the guard's compartment. A sack barrow is waiting ready for the Ryde train.

George H. Hunt

Wroxall Station, 1933, by Jimmy James

No. 30 *Shorwell* enters Wroxall Station from Shanklin in June 1965. Signalman Unstead is ready with the single line staff in his hand. The station housed a small lever frame. The ivy-covered building adjacent to the station was a hotel which provided the station refreshment room.

Dr Gerald R. Siviour

working at Merstone each day during the Summer service was the passing of the East-West limited stopper, 'The Tourist'. This was hauled by the bigger Brighton 'E1' class. She ran straight through non stop, passing at about 45mph, I would hold up the Merstone – Shide hoop while I would have to catch the brass staff. This felt like a hard schoolmaster's cane across the hand! It got so bad with my hands being cut badly that I had to complain and ask them to slow down to the proper speed of 15mph rather than 45mph.

It was essential to keep things running, but one morning I had a very awkward driver down from Newport shed shunting sugar beet with one of the bigger Brighton 'E1' engines. This held up the train from Sandown on which the district inspector was travelling. When he arrived at Merstone, this inspector pulled me over the hot coals about holding up his train at Horringford and wanted to know why. Of course, I had to tell him about the awkward loco driver. 'I'll put him in his place,' said the inspector. He came up in the box and made this engine do half an hour's unnecessary shunting up and down and in and out of sidings.

Generally, footplate crews liked to work at Merstone. They would go down the Ventnor West Branch, and call off on the way at Farmer Cheak's fields to pick mushrooms. During World War II we had a Spitfire shot down just two hundred yards away, if that. The Polish pilot parachuted out but was promptly arrested by the Home Guard who thought he was a Nazi pilot.

At Merstone Station, we had a level crossing and a subway which was 90 per cent of the time under water. This of course was used to our advantage. We pumped this water up into the loco water tanks which held something like 2000 gallons. Len Creath, the Outside Works man was in charge of these pumps, and we had to start them up by a large handle. On many occasions the handle would fly off! Very often the whole line between Merstone and Sandown would be flooded by the local river during the winter. Instead of train transport they have had boats out floating above the railway track.

At the conclusion of the War, I was transferred back to Sandown, where I had started my railway career. Whilst I was learning the signalbox at Sandown under the direction of George Wright we had a mishap with an engine off the road. The train had entered Sandown Station from Merstone, and the engine ran around the train after taking water, via the main line. At the Brading end of the station, she waited to join the other end of her train out on the main line. I didn't quite pull the point fully across but fireman Bob Church heard the point movement, didn't wait for the dummy signal to pull off and told the driver he had the right of way. Of course the loco came off the catch points.

How do you exchange tokens when you already have a train on one platform? Signalman Dick Randall shows how, as he passes the token to driver Jack Bradford on engine No. 36 *Carisbrooke* entering Wroxall with the 11.44a.m. to Ventnor on 13 July 1963.

John Goss

Early morning trains passing at Wroxall in June 1965, with No. 21 *Sandown* awaiting the path to Ventnor. From Wroxall the landscape changed as the chalk downs closed in around the line, which continued to climb at a gradient of 1:88 up to St. Boniface Down Tunnel.

Dr Gerald R. Siviour

Conversation at Wroxall between Signalman Dick Randall and Fireman J. Perkins. No. 31 *Chale* had been double headed on the 7.40a.m. Ryde – Ventnor train as far as Shanklin on 30 August 1965.

John Goss

Ventnor Station Terminus with '02' No. 28 *Ashey* in the platform, seconds before departure for Ryde Pier Head. The station and yard were built in an area literally blasted out of the hillside, 294 feet above sea level. Several sidings were provided for local goods, and coal merchants sub-leased the local caves in the hillside from a Ventnor railwayman as storing places for their merchandise. Note the solidly built goods shed adjoining the station buildings on the main platform — which was separated from the island platform by a single track. Not often used, the outer face island platform was reached by a small gang-plank.

R. J. Blenkinsop

Percy Primmer

I started work at Ventnor Town Station in 1929, and can well remember the 'Five Minute Bell' in use. You will of course be aware of the steep approach to Ventnor Station, and as far as I know, the practice of ringing a large hand bell outside the station, five minutes before the departure of a train, was done for the benefit of those intending passengers still coming up the hill. As far as I know, the bell remained at the station until closure. The menacing sound of the bell would give heavily laden tourists weighed down with luggage a minor heart attack as they panicked to struggle up to the station!

Perhaps not so well known was the unusual conveyance used to carry invalid passengers from the train to the taxis

at Ventnor Town. The Royal National Hospital for Diseases of the Chest was located at Ventnor. As a result we had plenty of invalids to cope with at times. However, instead of having a wheelchair as is in use at most terminal stations today, we had a chair with four short legs and four handles, two at the front and two at the back, rather like a sedan chair, but without the covered top to it. Two porters were needed to use it, and carried the passenger much as in a sedan chair. I well remember conveying the late Ralph Vaughan Williams, the composer, in this way.

One item of unusual equipment you may have heard of, is that of the portable footbridge at Ventnor Town Station until the closure in April 1966. It was positioned when in use between platforms one and two. The bridge was a very cumbersome affair and required two men to

A general view of Ventnor Station from the Downs above the tunnel. The station was opened on 10 September 1866 and closed on 18 April 1966. No. 24 *Calbourne* is waiting to shunt an additional coach on to the five bogies standing at the outer face of the island platform. Platform awnings were of corrugated iron and glass on wooden pillars, the roof over the main platform being in three distinct sections, as can be seen in the picture. The station buildings had a slate roof and the walls had an external rough cast finish. A helpful photograph for IOW railway modellers.

Ron Childs

put it into place There was an interesting procedure in using the footbridge, which was only introduced in about 1936; there was a bell code in conjunction with the signal-box situated at the entrance to the tunnel, because the bridge would be across the main running line. If there was a train waiting to depart in the number two platform, which could not leave until after the incoming train had arrived in number one platform, then obviously the bridge had to be removed at a given time. So before the signalman would accept a train from Wroxall, he would ring a bell on the platform and the bridge would be removed. We would then ring a repeating bell indicating the bridge had been removed. All was then clear for the arriving train.

The old bridge was wide enough to take a four wheeled luggage truck, and on more than one occasion, I remember a heavily laden four wheeled flat luggage truck sinking through the boards. I recall heaving a truck loaded with canned meat across to a luggage van on the other platform. Suddenly, the whole lot disappeared before my eyes! Splintering wood and cascading tins echoed around the white chalk cliffs which surrounded the station. This resulted in hurried unloading and dismantling before the next train was due.

Mention of the chalk cliffs around the station at Ventnor brings to mind the caves. These were used for many years as store depots for coal merchants, but during the last War they were used as air raid shelters for staff and nearby residents — particularly during the bombing of the radar station at the top of St. Boniface Down.

A very unusual incident happened on the first day of the Summer service of 1936 or 1937. The porter/signal-man, whose name was Jim Gladdis, at Ventnor Box, let the train from Wroxall in on to number one platform where another train was waiting to depart, instead of letting the incoming train into number two platform. The driver, Perce Toogood, had no reason to think that anything was wrong. As he came out of the tunnel he was

Engine No. 20 *Shanklin* bursts out of Ventnor Tunnel with a train from Ryde Pier Head in 1928. The signalman has set the three way point for Platform 1 and is in the process of accepting the token.
George H. Hunt

Signalman Harold Fry (left) and Inspector Ron Russell pose at the top of the steps at Ventnor Signalbox on 8 June 1964.
R. J. Blenkinsop

Below: The Ventnor Tunnel incident (*see Page 46*)

Inside Ventnor Signalbox. A pair of colour light signals inside the tunnel controlled access to the platforms.

R. J. Blenkinsop

suddenly confronted with a locomotive and train in his path waiting to depart. Toogood put on the brakes for all he was worth and managed to stop ten feet away from the other engine. When he climbed down off the footplate of the '02' tank, his face was as white as a ghost. The porter/signalman left the signalbox that day and never returned to the job again! On the train as a passenger was Ron Tewkesbury the carriage lighting officer at Ryde St. John's Road.

When I was in the parcels office at Newport, a ram arrived one day from Freshwater. It had come over on the car ferry via Lymington – Yarmouth, and then by train to Newport. There it was in the guard's compartment of a Chatham carriage, in number two platform. I couldn't move the ram; I pulled and tugged and had to give up. In the end I got hold of a four wheel luggage trolley and put the ram inside, wheeled it over the crossing and tied him up in the parcel's office. I phoned the farmer, and presently he arrived at the station with a small child. I untied the rope, the child caught hold of the rope and away he went.

Jack Collard

My father was the assistant stationmaster at Victoria and my mother also worked on the railways. It was natural then that I should join the railway and follow in their footsteps. I came across to the Island during the War, when my family moved to Freshwater to live. My job was booking clerk at Ventnor Station on alternate turn with an old chap called Westmore, and later Des Boynton took his place. The job involved ticket work, parcels, passenger luggage in advance work; there were often three full vans of luggage per day.

In those days at Ventnor we used to have a lot of fun. There were a lot of empty crates to return on the trains and one day I nailed one down to the floor. When Des Boynton came in to load up the crates on to the Ryde train he found he had problems. The following week when I was early turn, I opened the booking office and spotted a half crown coin on the floor. However, when I picked it up, I discovered it was a milk bottle top. On the reverse side of the top was an inscription 'Ever been had before — Des Boynton'. It was a perfect rubbed representation of a coin.

We used to have all sorts of things left in the carriages of trains that were found at the end of the journey at Ventnor. One day I found a portable gramophone on the carriage compartment rack which I put away in the office. On the next train down we discovered some records — just coincidence, I suppose.

I remember one day during the early fifties two plain clothes railway detectives came down to Ventnor — a young lady and a man, so as not to arouse suspicion. They sat together on top of the Downs, had a picnic and looked down on the station. We often used to have railway photographers and enthusiasts taking pictures from the top so we paid little attention. In fact they observed a man stealing coal from the wagons in the siding opposite the signalbox. They walked down, arrested him and he was convicted of theft.

We quite often managed to win the coveted 'Best Kept Station' competition. Tidiness and station gardens were taken into consideration, and a special seat was presented to the winning station on the Island which recorded the winner's name and year. Alec Widger used to bring across hanging baskets and flower tubs which made the station colourful and attractive to visitors. There were two clerks, a porter/signalman, two signalmen, a porter and the stationmaster at Ventnor and we all worked together to keep the station in good shape.

During the Summer season one day a chap slipped and broke his neck on the Downs above the station. Being a qualified first aider, I went up with a colleague, Charlie Puck, and we carried him down to safety. For this act I was taken to Waterloo and awarded a special commendation for saving his life.

After the 11.10a.m. arrived each day at Ventnor, Alec Widger would religiously walk down from his signalbox, collect some coal from the coal store at the back of the station, and leave the full bucket at the end of the platform. He would then call into the office in the station for his 'elevens'. On one particular occasion

Mad Jack Sturgess drove in the 11.10a.m. train on his engine No. 22 *Brading*. Now Jack had observed this ritual of Alec's for some time. This time old Jack Sturgess emptied the bucket of coal into his bunker on the engine. He then placed two cast iron chairs in the bottom of the bucket. Crafty Jack then filled up the remainder of the bucket with coal. Some minutes passed and Alec emerged from his coffee break in the station, picked up the bucket and staggered back to the signalbox with it. When he discovered what the contents of the bucket were Driver Sturgess was temporarily confined to the Cowes Road for a few days.

Tony Edmunds

I didn't particularly want to work anyway. I was vaguely aware at the age of 15 in 1942 that something would have to happen, but there was an extremely interesting war going on, and as all or most of the lads in Bembridge were either in the services or Woodnutt's boat yard and as my father had been employed at the latter man and boy, I assumed that it was there that my destiny lay.

School (Ryde Upper Grade) was acceptable, but I was certainly no academic, keeping in the A forms by the skin of my teeth. Fortune had smiled, however, insofar as my appetite for football and cricket was insatiable and that, combined with the frequent lengthy periods in the air raid shelters, passed the time quickly enough.

It was my mother who shook me out of my pleasant lethargy. 'You will have an office-job' she said. 'A steady job with a pension. I have written to Mr Lee (dear old Walt!) at the station.' And that was how it all began.

The whole of Bembridge in those days looked upon Walter Lee as the stationmaster, which of course he wasn't. If pressed as to his designation he would admit to being 'Clerk in Charge', a status which is probably still being hotly disputed between him and Charlie Wetherick, should the pair of them still be engaged in running an ethereal station either up above or down below!

My mother's letter must have been passed by Walter to higher authority at Brading, and life took a very serious turn when a reply was received summoning me to interview by Mr Martin at Brading Station on a Friday evening at 5.15 in March 1942. The 'summons' was signed by none other than C. F. de Pury, and what was more, attached to it was a free pass from Bembridge to Brading and return!

My mother made sure that I departed on the 5p.m. train from Bembridge on the fatal day. I have a feeling even now that I wasn't trusted not to leave home in the direction of the station, walk along the beach for an hour and report back fictitious failure.

The train reached Brading faster it seemed than it had ever done before, and there I was clad in my best grey flannels and blue sports jacket standing in the booking hall; mercifully the whole place appeared locked and untenanted. Suddenly the booking office 'clap' opened and I came face to face with the man who, there can be little doubt, must be haunted by the fact that he ever saw fit to recommend that I be employed by the Southern Railway Company.

I remember adopting a rather defensive, probably even truculent attitude, and was not surprised when Stan Martin suddenly said that a train left for Bembridge at 5.30 — I was away like the proverbial robbers' dog. As the train was pulling out a face appeared at the carriage window — it was Stan. 'What sort of job had you in mind,' he shouted. 'A clerk,' I shouted back. Blessed release.

But wheels were grinding rapidly and the next summons was to an interview at London West, Divisional Headquarters at Woking. During a casual chat to a fellow villager Roger Bartram I learned that he was due to undergo the same experience on the same day. Roger had a slight advantage in that he had some idea of the fate in store because his mother was booking clerk at Bembridge in the early war years (in place of Walt Lee who was suffering from a prolonged bout of something-or-other), and his elder brother John was in the B. O. at Portsmouth Harbour. Armed with almost identical letters, again signed C. F. de Pury, and identical free passes from Bembridge to Woking, we set off together and were duly interviewed in one of the green wooden sheds by the chief staff clerk — a Mr Cheeseman I think. This ordeal was over for both of us in about twenty minutes, and as we stood on the platform discussing the possibilities of success or failure, a train arrived and we got in. Once on the move Roger was sure that we were on the wrong train whilst I was adamant that we were not. Proof positive was when, after a stop or two we decided to check on our exact whereabouts with a member of the station staff. 'This is Aldershot,' he said. Eventually we returned to Bembridge, but I've often thought since about that day. It was significant insofar as I'm not sure that I managed to get my railway career exactly on the right lines from that special day until I resigned more than 11 years later. One thing however is undeniable: from those days (when the word industry had no application, for the railways were a service) stemmed friendships which have matured with the years, a maturity that is perhaps best assimilated rather than described.

Success at interview was followed by written examination at Southampton Central where again Roger and I got the nod, and were then invited to prove our physical fitness to a chap who rejoiced in the title of Medical Officer to the Southern Railway at London Bridge; how were we to get there we wondered, but Mrs Bartram came to the rescue and duly delivered us on time — 12.15p.m. The M. O. was morose to say the least and made it plain that his lunch was more important than checking out a couple of 15 year olds, but he gave us a pretty thorough going over and eventually pronounced, I thought reluctantly, that we would do!

A further brief interview with Stan Martin indicated that we 'were in', one to start at Sandown the other at Shanklin, and 'had either of us a preference?' I didn't particularly want to work anyway, but Roger did and opted for Sandown, and so we next met over the 8.22 a.m. from Bembridge on Monday 22 April 1942. On arrival at Shanklin on that day I waited until the

The lower quadrant signal gives the right away to a Ventnor bound train in 1928, but there is still luggage and parcels to be loaded aboard. Note the luggage trolley that has fallen off the platform in front of a wagon in the goods shed.

George H. Hunt

Ventnor Station by Jimmy James

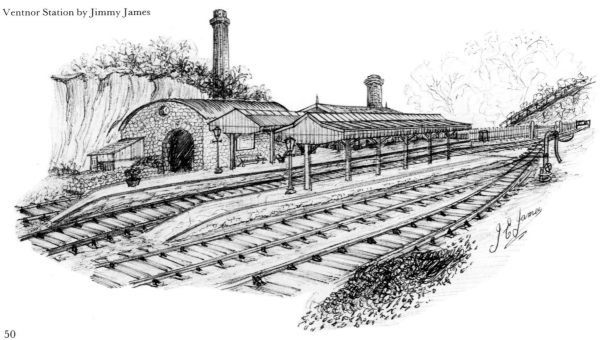

Ventnor Station desination board on 1 October 1965.

Peter J. Relf

Ventnor clock which dates back to the station's opening in 1866. It was maintained by Mr T. A. Awty of Freshwater.

R. J. Blenkinsop

Fireman Jim Moody takes on water for No. 20 *Shanklin* at Ventnor Station in 1964.

Dr Gerald R. Siviour

passengers had left, timidly approached the chap who was collecting tickets and asked for the stationmaster. 'That's me,' he said, and that meeting was the commencement of a relationship which ripened over the years until Walter Lown's death more than three decades later. (His great love in retirement was Shanklin Cricket Club for whom I played in the 60s and 70s, and no spectator was more pleased than Walter if I should get a 50 or a wicket or two).

I was ushered into the booking office and introduced to the lady charged with my induction into the secrets of life on the Southern Railway, Miss Beatrice Thick. 'Don't get wrong ideas because you're working with a lady. She will only have to shout to her father who is manager of the bookstall.' Through the window father Thick appeared as a portly, busy little man in his late fifties or early sixties with a small white moustache and a pork-pie hat which never left his head. Subsequently I noticed that he was continually redisplaying magazines as though ensuring that WHS did not purvey anything of which he might not approve.

It must have soon become apparent to the stationmaster that he did not have a born railwayman on his hands. There were two 'thicks' in the office, one who was obviously in total control of the job, and myself.

After a day or two the stationmaster came into the office and in the course of conversation I learned that pay day was Thursday, and that my rate was seven shillings and sixpence per week for the first six weeks. How incredible now, that throughout the whole recruitment process remuneration had not been mentioned. I felt soon that my cash-handling wasn't bad, the mathematics were no trouble, but I was petrified at the thought of timetable enquiries; even to accurately ascertain the departure time of the next train to Wroxall or Sandown was an achievement—except for the 4.42p.m. to Brading which meant release from purgatory.

Walter's son, Young Walter, then at Ryde Pier Head and now I suppose retired or about to after being promoted to the higher echelons at I think Victoria, did his best to assist me with train enquiries. 'Give me the train times,' he said, 'leaving Newcastle at 8a.m. to Truro via Crewe, Reading, and Guildford, and I'll be back in 20 minutes.' The books covered light blue, dark blue, green

and brown were complete mysteries; I couldn't have worked that trip out in a fortnight, let alone 20 minutes.

Somehow the six weeks passed and for reasons best known to Walter senior I was not fired but transferred to Ryde Esplanade where I was greatly privileged to meet some of the finest railwaymen I was to encounter in my comparatively short career. T. F. Thompson was stationmaster and in the booking office Fred Squibb, chief clerk, and Charlie Reeves. The two latter did their best to knock me into shape, Charlie sometimes literally. He was a 2nd Lieutenant in the Home Guard and I think felt he was fighting the War twenty four hours of each day on his own.

Both Fred and Charlie were inveterate pipe smokers, and it soon became obvious to me that 'if you want to get ahead—get a pipe!' I waited for my next pay day, went to Baxters on the Esplanade and bought a very nice little curled stemmed briar for one shilling and sixpence. Tobacco had to wait until the following week. Feeling quite manly I returned to work. 'What have you got there son?' said Charlie. 'A pipe Mr Reeves.' 'Got any tobacco? No? Then try some of this,' and he offered me his puche which appeared to contain nothing but black match heads. It was, I should have realised, navy brick readily obtainable from the naval chief and petty offices who regularly brought in the leave nominal rolls from H.M.S. *Medina* (now of course restored to sanity as 'Puckpool Park'). I was absolutely set up. 'Puff up,' said Charlie, handing me a box of matches, but I couldn't get the tobacco glowing and by this time I had an audience. 'Put some of this on top,' said Parcel Porter Charlie Jackson, and gave me some fine cigarette shag; this got the show on the road. I took about four puffs before the inevitable happened . . . Convinced though I was that nobody knew the reason for my dash outside perhaps it was not entirely coincidental that porters, Mrs House and Harry Driver, ticket collectors Frank Godsell and the two Charlies all enquired after my health, and having glimpsed my reflection in a mirror in the office why — my face was almost the same shade of green as the paint that Albert Watson's gang of lady painters was using on the station at the time. Nevertheless my pipe was a constant companion for the next 38 years.

'Would you mind helping out at St. John's Road?'

T. F. Thompson asked me one afternoon. 'John Richards the Junior Porter is sick; just collect tickets and look after the parcels office. Start at 7.30 tomorrow morning'.

It was at St. John's that I first encountered that, to me at least, most anomalous of all uniformed grades the Grade One Porter. Les Anderson was one such, and so high was the standard of his work that I couldn't comprehend why he was not a clerk. (In due course I was to be privileged to know others in this grade, or I think they were then - Harry Prangnell, Ron Coombes and Percy Primmer whose knowledge of and application to things clerical were of the highest order). Turn about with Les in the B.O. was Mrs Churchill, and it was Les to whom I reported on a miserable dark February morning. 'Your first job each day is the wagon return. Just go all round the yard, take the numbers of all the wagons. Note whether they are full or empty, then fill in the wagon return and send it to Ted Wheeler at Newport Office on the 8.50'. He handed me a book for the purpose.

I decided to start on the C.M.E. side of the yard, and found myself among some strange vehicles the names of which I had no idea. Their numbers did not appear in the book on the previous day, nonetheless I was determined to carry out my instructions to the letter when a voice rather curtly asked me what I was doing. 'Taking wagon numbers to put on the return for Mr Wheeler at Newport Office' I replied. Wally Herbert the C.M.E. foreman breathed fire - 'get out of my yard and tell Ted Wheeler that the breakdown-down train is no concern of his'. I felt distinctly unwanted and transferred my attentions to a siding near to the Loco. shed. Progress at last - all the wagons were clearly numbered, labelled 'loco dept.' and full of what was presumably steam coal; there were one or two here and there containing very 'small' coal. Suddenly an apparition was present. Never either before or since have I seen anyone so dirty black. The apparition in the form of Chaddie Willis, whose glass eye made him appear even more frightening enquired what I was doing; I launched into my 'taking wagons numbers' routine. 'I can't think' said Chaddie in his quiet voice, 'that you are meant to take the numbers of my dusters'. Lest he should have a change of heart I shot off to that part of the yard where the coal-merchants trucks of Wood & Co., Salter, Moore or Fountaine would, I hoped, present problems rather less complex. Les Anderson phoned the wretched return to Newport on the first morning due to my failing to meet the train departure deadline, and I soon concluded that the whole exercise was of limited value - at best the result hardly justified the effort required. How much easier it was particularly on a wet morning to sit in the signal box, drink a cup of tea with either Ron Jones or Vic Lacey (Sen.), and compile the damn return in comfort; it was possible to see most of the yard from there, and wagon numbers were for guessing anyway. My deceit remained undetected.

After a short while Mrs Churchill left, and I went into the B.O. on the opposite turn to Les. Clarence Jennings, later to die so tragically young, was transferred from the Pier trams (where he had been working as a conductor -

Basil Mattocks and Ray Barsdell were also there at about the same time along with the immortal pair of drivers Reggie Aylward and Jack Roberts) as Junior Porter.

St. John's was a busy place and there was usually someone other than station staff in the parcels office collecting mail from the box nailed on the wall. If it wasn't Harold (Shonko) Phillips, electrician, Jimmy James, carpenter, or Freddie Langton, plumber, it was one of their respective mates Jim Dibbens, Fred Calaway or Roly Drudge. 'Chancy' Wetherick, the C.M.E. clerk came in shortly after 8.00a.m. each day to collect mail with, I am sure, the same inexhaustible stub of a cigarette between his lips. Two occasional callers, probably to have 'priv' orders signed were Bill (Nobby) Clark (Newport Office) resplendent in the Sam Browne belted uniform of a lieutenant in the 'Hampshires' who always carried a most impressive walking stick, and Roy Whittinton (St. John's B.O.) who wore the white flash of an aircrew trainee in his RAF forage cap. Roy and I became quite firm friends possibly because I was keen to join the RAF, a step I am sure viewed as a relief from bondage. Roy longed to finish his training and be posted to a squadron which he accomplished, but alas was destined not to return from his very first operation over Germany.

Each morning the first train from Ryde left St. John's packed with workers at the Cowes munitions factories. The Workman's return fare was 1/6½d, and so many halfpennies did we have in the B.O. till that the only way to keep them within bounds was to give eleven as change from a 2/- piece which led to the occasional altercation with members of the travelling public.

The very mention of 'station coal' was sufficient, so to say, to generate considerable heat. I refer, of course, to the annual issue of house coal to the stations which was of doubtful quality and in quantity never enough to last the winter through. Shanklin was an unlucky station in this regard as their issue left Medina Wharf together with that for Brading and Sandown in the same truck, but by the time these two latter had guessed at and removed their allocations, what was left for Shanklin meant that the station staff there were the first to start scrounging buckets of steam coal. St. John's didn't have this problem as there was plenty of solid fuel to be had legitimately or otherwise, nonetheless Clarence Jennings treated the station issue as his and guarded it jealously. He once detected an unusually rapid depletion of his stock and nailed the blame firmly on the door of Ganger Charlie French without, as it transpired, very good reason.

Charlie had a double cross to bear. Firstly he had either a very strangely shaped roof to his mouth or his top teeth had been made for someone else; in any event the two were incompatible to such an extent that whenever he opened his mouth his top set descended on the bottom with a resounding click. When he spoke they made a noise like castanets, and it took a superhuman effort on his part not to fire them at anyone to whom he might speak. Rumours had it that he found this top set in the four-foot when walking the length one morning between St. John's and Brading after a particularly successful Ryde carnival procession.

Secondly, Charlie was Officer Commanding fire watchers with Headquarters in a padlocked goods wagon which reposed in a siding at the side of the Loco. shed nearest to the St. John's station buildings, and was heated by a tortoise stove, the chimney of which protruded through the roof. Each evening at about six o'clock Charlie would unlock the van and light the stove using, Clarence was convinced to the point of paranoia, 'his' coal. Shortly before six one evening, Clarence climbed on to the wagon roof and blocked the chimney with a wet piece of sacking, awaited Charlie's arrival, and, having given him time to light the fire shut the door and put the padlock through the staple. After a short while Clarence let Charlie out and retreated to the station buildings (in military parlance) 'under cover of smoke'. The whole exercise was something of a waste of time as the station coal continued to disappear.

Clarence continued to be the butt of practical jokers, and, having been round the yard one morning taking wagon numbers, he came into the B.O. muttering 'I'll have him, I'll have him'. It appears that as he was walking in the six-foot writing numbers in his book the fireman of a passing shunting engine had showered him with steam.

The following week I was late turn, and was surprised to see Clarence turn up one evening. 'Do you want to go the toilet?' (or something to that effect), he asked, 'not particularly' I replied, and he then outlined his plot.

The open end of the loco. shed faced south-west. The evening was quiet, almost balmy, with a slight breeze from that direction; the mess-room doors along the side of the shed were open.

'Did I want to go to the toilet now?' Clarence asked; and we went quickly and quietly to a point just outside the open end of the shed where in the six-foot was a heap of red-hot ashes recently drawn from a firebox upon which we both relieved ourselves. Never have I smelled anything quite so vile as the resulting acrid steam cloud which rolled gently on the breeze into the shed and into the open-doored mess rooms. One thing was certain, the flavour of that particular cloud of steam did not exactly act as garnish to the ritualistic cheese sandwiches and cold tea of which the victim was presumably partaking at the time. Doors were slammed shut in obvious high dudgeon, and by the time the mess-room occupants could open them without risk of further contamination both culprits had reached the safety of the B.O. Clarence considered honour satisfied.

The midday apple-core battle at St. John's Road became almost a part of station life. Again it was really a 'Clarence's revenge' situation, as apparently either a carpenter, electrician or plumber or a mate of the same had scored a bull's-eye on the back of his neck with an apple of indeterminate vintage, and so on this particular day, having collected a goodly assortment of ammunition ambush was laid and the villains awaited. They always came home for lunch on the up train - we knew more or less where they were working, and it so happened that no passengers, only the six alighted. Battle was joined. By force of superior logistics we drove them across to the down line where all escaped by taking advantage of cover

offered by the loop platform, all, that is, except plumber Freddie Langdon who concealed himself by standing behind a platform support stanchion, but it mattered not victory was ours. I had exhausted my ammunition, and Clarence had left only one small hard green apple which he threw with some force in a pretty desultory fashion in Freddie's general direction. By coincidental split-second timing the apple passed the stanchion at exactly the moment that the last of our enemies chose to put his head out to recce. There was a resounding smack as it struck Freddie on the right lower jaw; he left his cover, put his hands to his face and muttered as best he could that 'we had broken his false teeth'. As he passed through the booking hall on the way to his home in Daniel Street the grinding noises coming from his mouth confirmed this, and both clarence and I were, to say the least, more than a little concerned.

I saw him the next day, said how sorry we were and enquired about the state of his teeth. 'Oh, don't worry', said Freddie, 'they're mended'. Rumour had it that another of Len Creeth's many skills was that of dental mechanic.

So ended the last of the twelve o'clock battles and, come to think of it, there was little actual evidence of the damage; - I have a peculiar feeling that the last laugh was Freddie's.

Fred Perkins was the Travelling Auditor. A Chartered Accountant and hawk-nosed forbidding figure in dark suit, black overcoat and homburg, who always arrived at a station to do his stuff as the busiest train of the day was being booked.

One saturday morning Fred walked into the St. John's Road parcels office dressed in sports jacket and flannels and obviously not on an official visit. My clerical incompetence was still generally indisputable and I was wrestling blindly with a Parcels Daily Balance Book which had a will all its own and refused to accept the 3/4d worth of entries in any combination to which I subjected it.

Fred looked over my shoulder, explained how to solve my problem, and then said, 'always remember that where you have a debit you must also have a corresponding credit or credits'. The cloud lifted. This occurred more than 40 years ago as I write, yet it is as clear in my mind as though it were yesterday, possibly because I've been fortunate in being able to earn a reasonable living by virtue of applying 'Fred Perkin's Principle' for most of those intervening years.

The fact that I did some relief work at the Ryde stations was due, no doubt, to T.F. Thompson's acceptance of my many inadequacies, i.e. if I wasn't in the same place for too long the less chaos would result. Train enquiries continued to be my 'bete noir', although at the Esplanade the B.O. staff had clubbed together and bought an ABC which circumvented my fear and trembling to some degree.

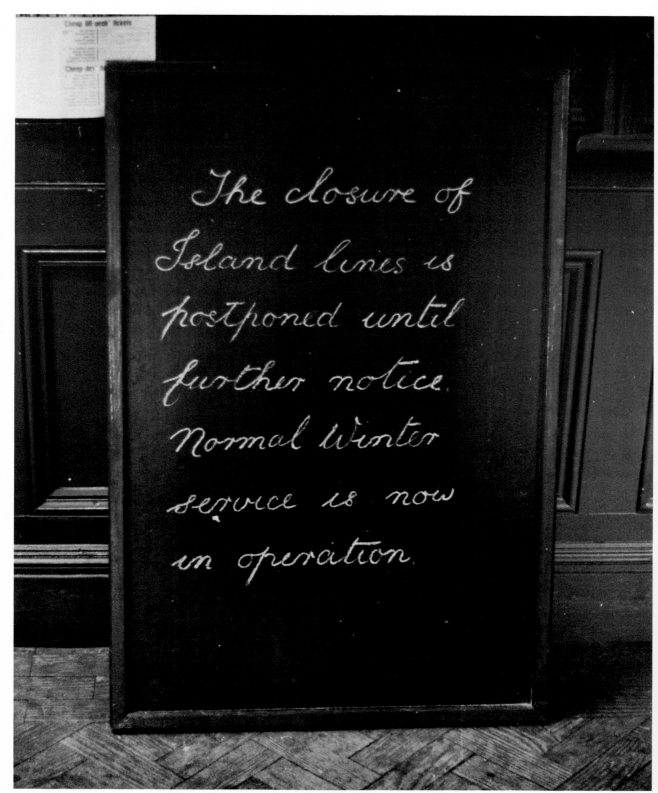

The closure of the Ryde – Cowes and Shanklin – Ventnor lines was planned for 4 October 1965, but was postponed pending an enquiry. This is the notice announcing that decision at Ventnor Station on 1 October 1965.

Peter J. Relf

Chapter Two ~ The Brading Harbour Branch
(Brading-Bembridge)

No. 15 *Cowes* sweeps around the curve into Brading with a train for Ventnor on Sunday 18 May 1952. Passengers changed here for St. Helen's and Bembridge — better known as the Brading Harbour Branch. The Branch opened on 27 May 1882 and Bembridge trains left from the island platform at Brading, accompanying the main line towards Ryde for a short distance before veering eastwards across the marshes.

Eric D. Bruton

The line followed a slightly serpentine course. Before reaching St. Helen's there were sidings for a brickworks and cement works — pictured here in 1936.

Timothy P. Cooper Collection

Pen and Ink Sketch of St. Helen's Quay by Jimmy James
Although quite extensive, St. Helen's Quay handled little traffic. The highlight of the Quay's history was in 1883 when an Isle of Wight Railway 2 – 4 – 0 Beyer Peacock tank engine *Bonchurch*, which was being landed, was dropped into the sea. It was recovered a few days later and ran for many years on the Isle of Wight!

St. Helen's Station in 1933 with a platform full of schoolboys awaiting the branch train to Brading.

George H. Hunt

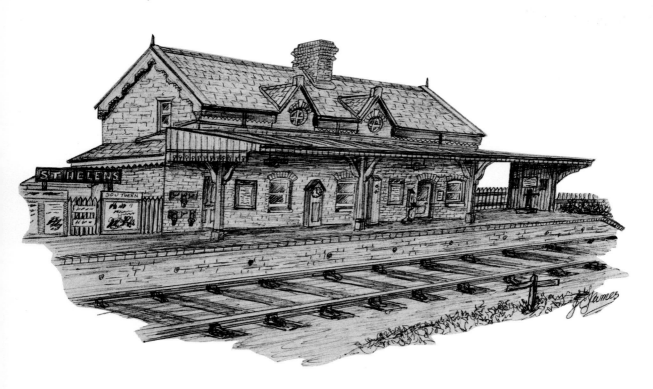

St. Helen's Station, 1933, by Jimmy James

Pen and Ink Sketches of Bembridge Toll Gate in 1934 and 1960 by Jimmy James. The road from St. Helen's to Bembridge also belonged to the railway and was operated as a toll road by the Railway Authorities.

Terrier tank No. 13 *Carisbrooke*, complete with copper capped chimney, at Bembridge Station in 1933. Pictured on the platform are left to right: Driver Bill Miller, Guard Rolly Buckett and Fireman Robert Beavis.

George H. Hunt

Bembridge Station, 1933, by Jimmy James

Chapter Three ~ The Newport – Merstone
Junction – Sandown Line

Shide Chalk Quarry, pictured looking down from the Newport Golf Course in 1936, just before the Sandown Line reached its first station at Shide on the outskirts of Newport. It had a branch which ran to a chalk quarry in St. George's Down.

C. G. Woodnutt/Timothy P. Cooper Collection

Shide Station in 1936. The red lamps on the crossing gates swivelled when the gates were opened so that they shone towards the road.

George H. Hunt

Following the success of the Ryde – Ventnor and Cowes – Newport lines, the next promotion was to construct a line from Sandown to Newport. The company constructing the line, the Isle of Wight (Newport Junction) Railway, experienced difficulties with the contractors and were only able to open the line from Sandown to Shide in 1875. The line was not extended into Newport until five years later; by that time the company was in the hands of the Receiver. Pictured, a train leaving Shide in January 1956.

Dr Gerald R. Siviour

No. 31 *Chale*, with Driver 'Toby' Watson at the controls, pulls into Blackwater Station in January 1956. The line ran level from Blackwater to Merstone Junction, through some delightful scenery. Sadly, the whole line between Newport and Sandown closed on 6 February 1956 (a month after this photograph was taken).

Dr Gerald R. Siviour

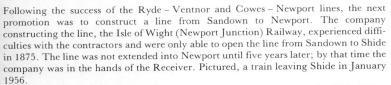

With the notice of closure prominently displayed on the platform of Merstone Junction Station, No. 25 *Godshill*, furiously blowing off steam, prepares to set off bunker first to Sandown.

Dr Gerald R. Siviour

Trains cross at Merstone Junction Station in January 1956. Driver George Ellis of Newport Shed, at the regulator of No. 33 *Bembridge*, makes a speedy departure with a two coach train for Newport and Cowes.

Dr Gerald R. Siviour

Edith M. Pragnell

I lived and worked at Blackwater Station, on the Sandown – Merstone – Newport Line, during World War II. My husband worked at Newport as a booking clerk, so we were really a railway family.

The service trains that did run were packed with war workers proceeding to or from the factories at Newport, Cowes and elsewhere on the Island. Lighting at night, was dimmed in the carriages, owing to the restricted lighting observations. Firemen on the footplate were ordered to keep their firehole doors closed as much as possible to avoid the glow of the fire being spotted by enemy aircraft. We were in the front line on the Island after the fall of France. I remember feeling very lucky at Blackwater, after hearing that Newchurch Station further down my line had been hit by a stray bomb. This had the immediate effect of closing our line between Newport and Sandown while repairs were carried out.

The only bad experience I had was when a goods train came crashing through the crossing gates, taking parts of them to the railway bridge further down the line. The driver was allowed to pass the distant signal, but was required to stop at the home signal. However, on this occasion he did not stop at the home signal, passing it at a fair speed! Mr Ern Landon, the inspector, came out from Newport to examine the damage and investigate. The shock of this incident frightened me so much that I had to give in my notice and leave the railway.

Memories of Merstone

It was on a Tuesday morning, one January day,
A party of Officials, came out Merstone way.
They travelled out by Taxis, shortly after Noon,
By train was out of question, as there wasn't any room.

They went into the Signalbox, found everything all right,
Till the Signalman looked up and said, 'Wot! no Electric Light.
Our Oil Stove is on repairs, has been for past two years,
If we couldn't see the funny side we'd be reduced to tears.

The welfare Gent from London, give the man his due,
Said 'We'll give you a new Oil Stove, without any more ado.
A Wash Basin we'll send you, (not giving any date),
And as regards Electric Light, we will negotiate.

Arriving at the Crossing gates, they thought they saw a drain,
But in fact it was a Subway, to keep people safe from trains.
If any hardy villager that way should enter in,
They'd be advised to bring Costumes, and make it with a swim.

Now one of our Officials, while peering in to see,
If Fate perchance would give him a tasty fish for Tea,
Saw Tadpoles, Tiddlers, Newts, and Frogs, in its mystic depths revealed,
When his pencil top from pocket slipped, and alas, its fate was sealed.
It dived into the water, with a splash and with a thud,
Till its silver beauty was begrimed, with 6 inches of mud.

The Staff all got together, to retrieve it they did try,
And ran the Engine for 3 days, to pump the Subway dry.
When after hours of searching, and raking with 6 toothed prong,
The missing pencil top was found, it was precisely 1 inch long.

But their efforts were rewarded, in spite of hours of toil,
And the Cost? 1 pint of 'Gaitskell's Pool', and 3 gallons of Oil.
The moral to this Story, you'll agree without a doubt,
Is, keep Pencil safe in pocket, in case there's Ducks about.

'Vecta'

Syd Dennett

My career on the Island railways began back in 1927 in Southern Railway days as a junior porter at Newchurch. After three years they offered me various vacancies such as a goods porter at St. Helen's Quay and a carriage cleaner at Effingham Junction, but I decided to stay on at Newchurch and see if anything better would come up. Eventually a grade one porter post came up at Horringford. My experience at Newchurch as a junior porter had been invaluable with the jobs I had to do such as issuing tickets, opening gates, answering the telephone, parcel work and goods work, and this was to provide a good foundation for my new responsibilities at Horringford. The new job entailed 50 per cent clerical work and 50 per cent signalling work with the gates. This gave me a taste for signalling work and I decided this was for me.

In 1940 I moved a little further along the line to Merstone Junction where the Ventnor West Branch diverged from the Sandown – Newport Line. Here I was porter, booking clerk and signalman. We had some fun and games at Merstone with the trains. There was a driver called Alec Bailey who was a regular driver on the Brighton 'Terriers' on the Ventnor West Line. One day Alec arrived into Merstone late from Ventnor West with the copper-cap chimney 'Terrier' No. 13 *Carisbrooke*. Well, I had already accepted a train from Shide, with the Newport – Sandown local. Alec shouted up to the box

that he had time to run round his train. As he moved forward out towards the Shide end he spotted the oncoming Newport – Sandown local approaching at speed down the end of the straight on the same line! Well Alec opened up that engine full regulator and the 'Terrier' tank shot down to the end of the platform where he applied the brakes. You have never seen an engine skid so far. Back he went on to the other end of his Ventnor West train waiting in the adjacent platform; and all was well.

On other occasions all did not go well. Inspector Henry Powers was entering Merstone Station on a Sandown – Newport train and he was travelling in the Guard's compartment of the front carriage next to the engine. The signalman, Jess Wheeler had just collected the single line staff from the fireman of the engine when Inspector Powers opened the door to alight. Well the door caught the unfortunate signalman on the face. Jess Wheeler let fly verbally at the inspector for his stupid actions. Later on Jess was up in the signalbox and the fire got down very low, so he threw some oil on the stove. There was a loud explosion which blew the chimney pipe away from the wall of the signalbox. Some days later Mr Fiddler came out to examine the damage, but Jess claimed that the explosion was caused by a build up of gas.

From October until the end of December we loaded sugar beet every day for the Yorkshire Sugar Company of Selby. Merstone was a very busy station during this

Merstone Station, 1920, by Jimmy James

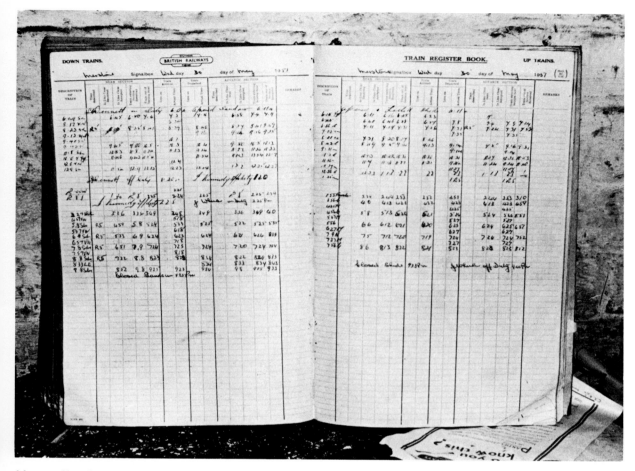

Merstone Signalbox Train Register Book.

H. Peter Mason

period of three months each year, with a nineteen wagon train for the Medina Wharf each day. One night after the final Ventnor West train had been put away into the siding for the night, the South Western '02' engine coupled up to the sugar beet wagons to haul them back to Newport. Unfortunately, the engine came in a bit hard and hit the trucks, causing the sugar beet to shower over the tops of the trucks. By sheer coincidence, that ill-fated guard Tom Courtney was standing beside the trucks. The beet rained down on him dirtying his immaculate uniform. A few nights after this, Toby Watson drove in with another South Western '02' and snatched the wagons of sugar beet out of the siding. He shot forward with just the engine and brakevan. What had happened was that as he snatched forward with the train the drawbar broke. There were red faces that night!

Generally, the drivers on the Ventnor West Branch were a good set of lads. Eddie Prangnell often used to come up into the box in between trains with his fireman for a cup of tea. I recall on one occasion upon returning to their engine No. 35 *Freshwater*, Eddie discovered that the fire was almost out. There was a mad panic and he

broke up some sleepers for wood to start the fire again. With just about enough steam to move, they staggered round the curve towards Ventnor West.

Some years earlier, I remember an incident involving the little Brighton Terrier No. 11 *Newport* at Merstone. In order to save time George Francis, the guard of the Ventnor West Branch train, disconnected the Westinghouse brake pipes on the carriage set for a quick shunt into the siding in front of the Merstone Signalbox. The lightweight Brighton No. 11 *Newport* pushed these carriages and when the time came to apply the brakes, the driver discovered there was nothing there to apply. The result of this was that the train crashed into a wagon between it and the stop blocks. The wagon which was loaded full of ash from the branch engines, careered over the stop blocks and exploded sending up a mushroom cloud of ash! My immediate concern was that the wreckage was not interfering with the main line. How they got away with that one I will never know.

Another incident involving that No. 11 engine was on a foggy morning before the Second World War. They had a relief signalman at Merstone at the time and I was on duty issuing tickets. Bill Dibden was the guard on the Ventnor West train, and Dick Hollands was the driver. After Dick had finished oiling up the little Brighton, the guard gave him the tip to go down to the end. It was the signalman's job to give a green flag from the box for the 'right away' and he had not done so. The engine started off and all six coupled wheels came off the road, along with carriage bogies and so on as they passed over the point work. This created a major line blockage for some hours.

Towards the end of the Ventnor West – Merstone and Sandown – Newport lines they would do anything to discourage trade. However, we still had a lot of pride at Merstone in our station, and for three consecutive years we won the first prize in Group Two for the Southern Region of British Railways — Best Kept Station. As yet on the booking side there was no cheap day return ticket from Merstone to Sandown. You had to take a monthly return for 1 shilling 10d. But you could purchase a 'cheap day' for 1s 6d to Wroxall two stations further on. It was things like that which stopped people using Merstone station. What they ought to have done was reduce the service during the winter, as they did during the fuel crisis, and just run morning and evening trains for people going to shops, offices and schools.

Two pictures of Grade One Porter, Syd Dennett, at Horringford St in the early 'thirties. The appearance of the station was a credit to h
Syd Dennett Col

Junior Porter, Syd Dennett, poses for the camera before opening Newchurch Station crossing gates in 1928.

Syd Dennett Collection

68

Horringford was a typical county station rarely used from 1934 onwards, probably because it was situated in an isolated position far from the village of Arreton — which I assume was where most of the passengers came from.

I never witnessed the spectacle, but I have been informed that in its heyday this small station was a hive of industry. It coped with the whole farming community thereabouts trekking to Newport on market days, and villagers travelling either to Newport or Sandown for shopping expeditions. At that time the station boasted a stationmaster, and a series of cattle pens. One thing it did not boast was running water. At the rear of the station were three cottages and situated in the garden was a well, from which water had to be obtained for all purposes.

There was one railwayman who did not realise that to get nice clean water from such a well meant lowering the bucket gently into the water. This gentleman dropped the bucket with such force that it quickly sank to the lower regions. When he eventually hauled it to the top, to his great consternation a toad jumped out of the bucket! As is imaginable the cottage residents were extremely annoyed. They said it would be probably two days before the water cleared enough to be usable again.

Jimmy James

Horringford Station by Jimmy James

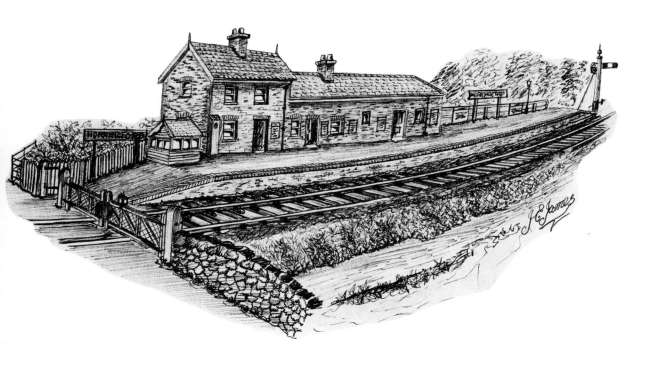

Ellen Wheeler

During the last war I had to register for work of national importance. As my husband was a regular serving soldier, and my only child was living with relatives near Oxford for the duration, I was available for full-time employment.

My first thoughts were to join the NAFFI as a cook, but my husband did not like the idea, so it was suggested to me by Reg Sheath, who was an auditor on the mainland for the Southern Railway, that I apply for a job on the Island Railways. My application was successful and I was sent to Horringford Station, on the Sandown – Newport Line as a grade one porter.

My first two weeks at Horringford were under the supervision of experienced railwaymen, and I was eventually passed out to take over by Mr Churchill, the area inspector. The duties involved operating the signals from the box on the platform, opening and closing the crossing gates by hand, general office duties of issuing tickets, booking up and cashing up which involved sending the cash to Mr Attrill who was stationmaster at Sandown. He only visited the station once a week to check that everything was in order, otherwise the running of the station was left to myself and the junior porter who worked alternate shifts to me.

The Southern Railway required me to work from 6.15 a.m. until 1.45 p.m. one week, and from 1.45 p.m. until 9.15 p.m. the next week, including Sundays. This seven day week working roster had no rest days, but we didn't get bored with the daily chores as we met all sorts of interesting people using the trains.

In those days the local farmers sent their milk in churns on the little green trains to Newport. There was also a tremendous amount of sugar beet grown in the Horringford area that was sent in trucks as far as Medina Wharf, where it was transferred to boat en route to Selby in Yorkshire for processing and refining. A regular job in connection with the sugar beet traffic was to label the wagons with the weight and destination and keep records of daily movements.

My favourite duty at Horringford Station was to receive consignments of day old chicks from a large poultry farm at Upwey near Weymouth. It was often late in the evening when they arrived at Horringford. We had orders from the stationmaster of Sandown to get the chicks to the people concerned that night as they required food and water. Some of the farms were half a mile away, and it meant walking instead of using my cycle if I had two boxes — one in each hand. The only consolation was that they were very light. We usually got a lot of thanks and a tip for our trouble so it was worthwhile, and all in a good cause.

During the War there were a lot of servicemen stationed at camps nearby who used the trains in the evenings when off-duty. They would often travel into Sandown to watch a Bette Davis film at the cinema, rushing on to the train at the last minute without tickets. Bearing in mind it was dark on the platform when they returned on the last train, due to the blackout and cars waiting for me to open the crossing gates, I had to collect the passengers' tickets as soon as possible. When the rush had died down on returning to the office, I then had to check the tickets carefully. Whilst sorting through I would regularly discover lots of pieces of cigarette packets cut to the same size as a ticket. This probably went on all over the place, I guess. Many of these soldiers joined the Island railways after the War and married local girls. Eddie Spears, the signalman, was one of them.

One dark night I had a scare after the last train had left for Newport and the station buildings were locked up. As usual, I hurried away towards the shed to collect my cycle to ride home, but on this occasion I tripped over something. In the darkness I timidly reached down to feel something which was soft and furry. Could it be a cat or dog I thought? At last I managed to grasp my cycle lamp. The beam of the light highlighted a very small badger which had hurt its leg and had a difficult job to crawl along. I managed to move the poor creature on to the siding. Several weeks passed and a fully grown badger was killed by a train on the line. A local farmer's wife had it skinned and cured to make a pram rug. I have often wondered if these unfortunate creatures were related.

My husband left the Army in March 1944 and started on the Island railways at Blackwater in April 1944, taking over from Mrs Prangnell who was leaving the railway. For a few months we both worked at stations on the same stretch of line. When I left Horringford in 1945, my husband took over my job — surely a unique occurrence. He stayed on the Island railways for 27 years, having worked as relief at different stations, and relief at Bembridge Tollgate. He eventually became a signalman at Merstone, then Haven Street and finally Brading. Sadly my husband died in 1974 at the age of 67 years.

George H. Hunt

Like so many Island railwaymen, my railway activities started on the mainland, at Southampton Terminus Station in April 1917 with the London South Western Railway. I had only been to the Isle of Wight on one occasion, and had seen nothing of the Island railways, so my promotion to the Island was a vast change in railway working from what I had been used to. Many of us from the old LSWR and LBSCR were sent to the Island to implement the eight hour day. All small stations usually had one resident stationmaster, with one relief for two stations, all working full day coverage for four days a week except Sundays. My arrival in the Island in June 1925 coincided with the period when the Southern Railway were making fundamental changes to improve the Island railways.

From Ryde Pier Head I travelled to Sandown, where I had to change for the Newport train. The stationmaster at Sandown was Mr Alec Wheway who was in attendance on the train from Ryde. As I was in uniform as soon as I alighted from the train he asked 'Another young man from the mainland. Where are you bound for?' 'Newchurch,' was my reply. 'Then come with me. I will escort you to your train' said Mr Wheway. Seated, he left me with the words, 'I wish you well. Your stationmaster is Dick Whittington.'

Newchurch Station in 1925. The waiting room on the left of the picture was the old signalbox from Mill Hill Station. The canopy part of the station was originally part of Pan Mill Station in Newport — which was the terminus of the IWNJR in 1879.

George H. Hunt

Newchurch Station shortly after re-building in 1930.

George H. Hunt

Newchurch Station, 1930, by Jimmy James

Upon alighting from the train at Newchurch, I wondered where I had come to! A single platform station, made of timber and ashes. The station buildings looked like a small goods depot. Newchurch was a Block Telegraph Post, with no control over the Train Staff and Ticket, for this was controlled by Sandown and Merstone Junction signalboxes. It was some years later that I learned the reason for Block Telegraph Post working.

The signal frame was in two sections, one part a small ground frame, and the other what must have been a shunting frame at some time. The adjusting screws on the signal wires, allowing for change in temperature, were very antiquated and our District Inspector told me if the signals did not come off to go outside and pull the wires. Distant signals at Newchurch, had no specs or lamps at this time; during darkness apparently the firemen were trained on location of these signals. They would shine their hand lamp to see if the signal was on or off. The goods siding was not suitable for engines to enter beyond a short way from the points so wagons were loose shunted, and, when empty, wagon levered back to the clearance point for picking up.

A few days after my arrival I was asked if I would go to Newport as a temporary guard, working trains between Newport, Freshwater, Cowes and Ryde. The old Isle of Wight Central Railway guards were supplied with a personal tail lamp, and as it had brass fitments they were kept in spick and span condition.

When working a train from Newport to Ryde Pier Head, a few days after starting as a guard, I arrived at Ryde Esplanade. When I left Ryde St. John's Road an old porter asked me if the Isle of Wight train was about. (Tradition dies hard.) I enquired, 'which Isle of Wight train? They are all Isle of Wight trains to me.' 'Oh no,' replied the porter. 'Your train is a Central one. The Isle of Wight Railway train is the Isle of Wight train. With that the porter loaded a barrow of parcels into my van. I was later told by another guard that if they lost a Newport train, this saved time for the Ventnor – Ryde train. The IWR trains were obviously more favoured.

Whilst at Newchurch, I had been chosen to be pilot-man on 8 December 1926 for the installation of the 'short and long staff' working on the Freshwater Line. At Freshwater there was a new signalbox and quite a lot of station improvements. The signalbox at Freshwater was a ground frame with ten levers with two spares. It wasn't long before I encountered a few problems. Fortunately Mr Urry, my stationmaster at my new post at Freshwater, said that if I found myself in difficulties and the ganger was about, he would most likely be able to help me out. The ganger, Tar Hetheridge, had during the 1914-18 War been a soldier in the Royal Engineers

(Transport) and acted as ganger on the Palestinian Railway. Not only did they have to know about track maintenance but also signal maintenance. I learnt a lot from him. After six months at Freshwater, I was promoted to signalman at Ventnor.

As Ventnor was of the old Isle of Wight Railway of course it was more up to datê. There were a few things worthy of mention about Ventnor in 1928. The telegraph wires went over the Downs over the tunnel and then back to the railway. Apparently in the days of the IWR the railway contracted the Post Office for the maintenance of telephone and Electric Train Staff equipment. It was cheaper and more convenient than employing their own staff for such a small mileage. I was informed by the older staff that two home semaphore signals were outside the tunnel, but this was not at all satisfactory because steam coming out of the tunnel mouth made it difficult for the enginemen to see them. The platforms were quite near, so eventually two colour light red/green signals were placed inside the tunnel. As there was a quarry adjacent, when any blasting had to be done, this was performed between train arrivals and departures and the signalman had to vacate the signalbox for safety.

I had a spell at Smallbrook Junction for the summer of 1929, but in November I transferred to Merstone Junction. The level crossing here was the only one in the Island worked by a wheel. Signalmen at crossing places, according to the Regulations, had to bring trains to a stand, or nearly to a stand, at the home signal, before pulling off the signal. I remember the District Inspector, when I passed for the box, informed me *not* to bring the trains to a dead stand if possible as it cost fuel — 1s 6d to start the train again.

I had one surprising experience soon after I arrived at Merstone Junction. I was sitting in the signalbox with the Ventnor West train waiting at the platform for the arrival of the Newport train to Sandown, when I heard a slow puffing. Looking out of the window, to my surprise I saw the Ventnor West train moving. Fortunately there was no traffic near the crossing gates so I opened up, and the train continued on its course at a snail's pace. The engineman had gone to the toilet, and the locomotive, a small Brighton Terrier (possibly No. 11 *Newport*), and the two push-pull carriages had gone. As leaving the station the line takes a severe curve the train had come to a stand. When the enginemen had brought the train back into the station, I enquired what was the reason. The red faced driver told me the small Brighton engine had centred, something he had not experienced before.

Jimmy James

The staffing of the remote stations on the Isle of Wight was often by young men who were in reality just commencing their railway careers. Two were employed on each station, one on early turn and one late. Supervision came from occasional visits by the stationmaster of one of the main stations.

Just for an example, there was Richard Russell — a keen young man who was based at Alverstone. An early turn of duty would comence quite early in the morning,

Stationmaster Richard 'Dick' Whittington at Newchurch Station in 1925.

George H. Hunt

Signalman George H. Hunt and Porter-Signalman W. Matchan at Newchurch in 1926.

George H. Hunt

Alverstone Station in 1932. The Drummond boilered '02' No. 28 *Ashey* barks out of the station and prepares for the steepest gradient on the line — rising for half a mile of 1:54 into Sandown Junction.

George H. Hunt

A series of cartoons by Jimmy James, who thought he would enjoy a few quiet days working at Alverstone Station, and was rather surprised to discover the reputedly quiet rural station was a hive of activity. The cartoons are reproduced by kind permission of Mr Richard Russell.

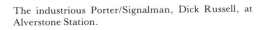

The industrious Porter/Signalman, Dick Russell, at Alverstone Station.

Jimmy James's private saloon carriage! Occasionally it did work on behalf of the Isle of Wight railways. For complete details of this Porcupine coach see page 94 of *Once Upon A Line* Volume One.

when he would prepare for a cycle journey of some four or five miles through country roads, and up many long hills. As often as not, it seemed it was raining and he would have to dress in oilskins and leggings. He would start on his merry way, arriving at his destination often dampened, but not dispirited. After unlocking the station and drying off a little, he would prepare for the first train of the day by opening the four crossing gates and operating the signals. The thought would pass through his mind that if it were not for trains the job would be quite easy! However, after the train had gone he would commence his mundane duties: clean the fireplace in the Waiting Room, lay and light the fire, after trailing outside again to fetch coal. Following this he would wash the Waiting Room floor, then there would be a quick cleaning of the windows. Oil lamps had to be cleaned and refilled, which meant a fair journey up and down the track to distant signals; and the wetter the weather the more distant they seemed.

Between all this labour of course, trains and passengers would come and go; there was no end to it. Of course Richard did snatch five minutes to have a cup of tea, but the break gave him a chance to look dejectedly at his Waiting Room floor where people had been shaking their wet clothes all over the place. It would just about cap it all when his late turn relief arrive and said, 'I thought it was your turn to wash the floor today!'

Andrew Britton

Jimmy James was one of the Isle of Wight railway carpenters. During his service he worked at every Island station and signalbox. Whilst working at his trade in contact with Island railway staff, he became a keen observer of human behaviour. With his sense of humour and artistic gift, the result was the frequent appearance of comic sketches, cartoons of interesting personalities, and the amusing situations of a busy life on the Island railways.

Today Jimmy James' original cartoon drawings are much valued and appreciated by railway enthusiasts. He has been kind enough to make a contribution of his particular style of railway art, to be included in this book. In view of the fact that Mr James is now suffering from cataracts of the eyes this has involved considerable effort. At first Mr James felt unable to undertake this task, but after repeated requests from his former colleagues and railway enthusiasts he has generously supplied the cartoons contained in this book.

Draughty places, booking offices, especially hazardous when you were waiting for hard earned wages to be paid through them.

The local railway station certainly had its place in community life!

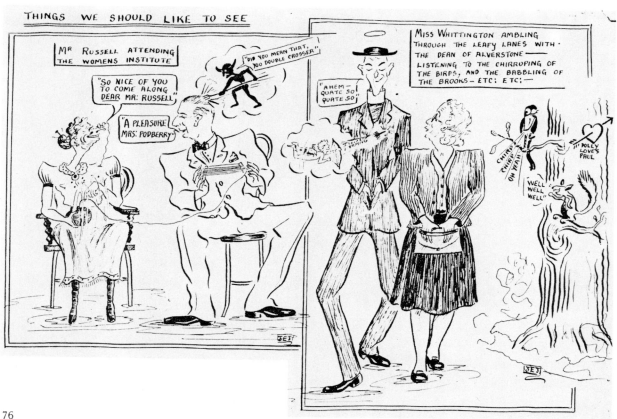

Could this have been a staff bonus for railwaymen at Alverstone?

Many stories of life in the signalboxes on the Island railways concerned animals and birds. Firstly, there was the station cat at Sandown. Very artful this one, calling at the signalbox for milk, then the porter's room, and then the booking office. He would jump under trains entering and leaving the station and come up the other side having narrow escapes most days. He would get among the trucks during shunting operations and although most of the staff were wise to it he frightened some of the passengers waiting for their trains on the platform. After all that the cat died of cat flu! The chap who had the job of burying him on a piece of spare ground put up a cross and epitaph as follows: 'Here lies the body of poor 'Tiger Tim' — the trains all missed him but the flu got him.'

Then there was the time I went on late turn at Sandown Box and found a live owl sitting in the corner. I never did find out who was responsible for that!

At that time Syd Dennett, the signalman at Merstone on my turn, had a pigeon named Bill. This bird would go to work with him each day, either perched on his shoulder as he cycled down the road or fluttering along just behind. It was Syd's practice on the early turn to shut Bill up in the brake van of the early goods train, with instructions to the guard to let him out at Sandown to fly back to Merstone. This went off all right for a time, until one morning Syd rang up asking where Bill was. 'On the station roof,' I replied. 'Well chase him off,' said Syd. This I did, but Bill flew round for a few minutes and took up the same position. Then, when the Newport train ran in he jumped on to the roof of one of the coaches and had a ride back to Merstone. He never did fly back again but just waited for the next train. One morning he even rode back on the roof of the driver's cab of the engine. I expected him to take off when the train got down round the corner, but he stuck it out all the way to Merstone. Syd got fed up with sending him after that.

We sometimes had a consignment of calves from the mainland which came on one of the early trains from Ryde, and they had to be transferred to the train for Merstone. They were nice little creatures and as they had rope halters on we used to lead them round like dogs one at a time. Then one of the Merstone guards decided he could take two. He had got them nearly to his train when something frightened them and they bolted, one going one side of a post and the other around the other side, doing considerable damage to the guard's nose. He never tried that again.

We once had a failure of the Token Instruments between Ryde St. John's Road and Brading on a dark, wet winter's evening. The lineman could find nothing wrong with either instrument and decided there must be a fault on the line between the two. At that time we had copper wires high up on poles. In Whitefield Woods he found a pheasant had caught a foot in a wire, and in his struggles to escape had gone over and over, twisting two wires together and was hanging upside down by one leg.

When I was at Alverstone, we had a mystery of various drivers reporting a cow on the line near Sandown Water Works, but when anyone went down there, no cow was observed on the line and no holes in the fence. I solved that one by lying in wait one afternoon. I discovered that one cow in the herd was a jumper. It would jump the fence and jump back again when it was ready. After that the farmer kept it in a field well away from the railways.

My last animal story concerned the rabbits at Medina Wharf. While working there as a checker one day, I emerged from behind a wagon to be nearly shot by a grade one porter who thought I was a rabbit. By the way, the rabbits there were black in colour. That was not their natural colour, but they were made black by the coal dust.

Sandown was a very interesting job from the signalman's point of view, but a very busy one when all the lines were open. When a train ran in from Ventnor and Shanklin to go through to Merstone and Newport, the signalman had to show the driver the Sandown – Merstone staff, 'give him the the Sandown – Merstone ticket and collect the Shanklin – Sandown staff from him. That took some getting used to. We had a bit of fun working there. Once a week we had a beer van from Cowes. It would arrive on the front of a passenger train next to the engine, and after the engine had taken water, it would have to be shunted to the down siding before the return journey to Cowes. This of course had to be done in between the normal up and down Ventnor trains. The beer was delivered to the local pubs next morning and the empties loaded into the van ready to go back by goods train. It used to be said that that particular train from Cowes had more beer on board than any of the crack named expresses on the mainland.

We also had milk vans at Sandown on the Newport trains. The milk in churns would be loaded at Merstone (most of this would have come from the Ventnor West Line), Newchurch and Alverstone. This milk was for Portsmouth and if the van was on the front of the train, the Newport engine would take it up into the Shanklin section and run it back on to the rear of the Ryde train. Alternatively, if it was on the rear, the Ryde engine would uncouple and go in and collect the van, and shunt it back on to the front of its own train.

There was also flower traffic from Newchurch to Covent Garden. The flowers were packed in cardboard boxes, but there were no special vans for these. They were loaded in the trains vans, sometimes up to the roof, hardly leaving room for the guard to get in, and all these had to be transferred to the Ryde train at Sandown. Officially there was only one porter to do this, but I have sometimes known nine chaps working away at it. I have known the porter (whose job it was) the signalman (me), the driver, the fireman and guard of the Ryde train, the driver, fireman and guard of the Newport train together with the chap out of the parcels office, all mucking in to keep delays to a minimum, and to get the flowers to Covent Garden on time.

While at Sandown, I had a total failure between Sandown and Shanklin. The block instruments were dead as were all the telephones. I found out why when a member of the permanent way department came up and said, 'I don't know if it makes any difference to you or not, but we have been lopping trees and a branch has fallen down

Alverstone Station by Jimmy James.

No. 29 *Alverstone* approaches the end of its journey from Newport, as it rounds the curve into Sandown, in January 1956.

Dr Gerald R. Siviour

through all the telegraph wires.' Needless to say, it did make a difference!

We had some laughs at Sandown. I can still laugh thinking about the porter assisting with shunting in the outside road over the Newport side. He jumped up into the brake van with such force he went straight through and out the other side and rolled down the bank. He climbed back a few minutes later, scratched and stung by nettles, but otherwise unhurt. Another one, about the same time jumped up from the track on to the platform, hit his chin with his knee and knocked himself out. There were several cases of the fireman of the Newport train omitting to couple up, and the engine going out leaving the train behind.

For a time my younger brother was signalman at Brading and lived at Sandown, and I was signalman at Sandown and lived at Brading. We used to pass each other on our bikes about half way when going to work, and going home from late turn about midnight. It was during this period we had a train from Ryde on Saturday afternoon which terminated at Sandown. The engine ran round its train and left from the down main, through the crossover to Brading, where the train was berthed in the Chalk Siding and the engine went back to Ryde St. John's Road. This took place as usual one Saturday and a couple of hours later a man called out to my brother at Brading Box, 'Where is that train going that's up the siding?' On being told, 'Nowhere until tomorrow morning,' he said, 'Well, there's an old lady sat in it.' The stationmaster was called, and he went up with a ladder and got the old lady out and back to the station. It seems she was for Wroxall, and had gone through the barrier at Sandown and got on the train after the guard and station staff had made sure the train was empty. She was quite happy, and when the stationmaster asked her if she thought it strange, she said she thought they were put in the siding to let another train go past. She must have seen many trains go by while she was there, but she didn't seem to mind. Just for the purpose the next down train terminated at Sandown, and the one after that terminated

at Shanklin, so we reckoned it took her about four hours to get from Sandown to Wroxall. Some sort of a record here?

Another story concerning Brading involves Mr Cotton, a fishmonger from Ryde, who went to Brading each Wednesday and did his rounds with a two wheeled barrow. He used to load up his barrow into the guard's van at Ryde Esplanade, and usually did a bit of filleting during the journey to save time. One morning the train gave a lurch entering Brading Station upsetting the barrow, scales, greaseproof paper, etc. There was then a mad scramble to get it all picked up and out on to the platform. After the train had left for Sandown Margie Cotton realised the weights which went with his scales were still in the van. Of course he could not do his rounds without them. The signalman phoned Sandown and said 'Margie Cotton has left his weights in the van.' The message came back that they could not be found. The same thing happened at Shanklin, and then it turned out they had all been looking for a packet of Player's Weights cigarettes. The weights had to come back from Ventnor before he could start selling any fish.

When I first came to Ryde St. John's Road, I discovered the most interesting part of the year was the opening and closing of Smallbrook Junction Signalbox. Smallbrook was only open for the summer months and then we were double line from Ryde Pier Head to Smallbrook. The signalman at Smallbrook had all the decisions to make, and he could either keep the job running smoothly or mess things up completely. I had a couple of summers there and although it was a lonely job I quite enjoyed it. There was no water, gas or electricity laid on there. We had a water can we would send in to Ryde St. John's Road on the last engine each evening, and the signalman there would fill it up and send it back the next morning. I have done many a turn of duty there without seeing anyone apart from people going by in the trains. I never minded that but it used to get some of the chaps down a bit.

'E1' No. 3 *Ryde* marshalls the school train at Sandown, just before 8 a.m.

Dr Gerald R. Siviour

Chapter Four ~ The Ventnor West Branch
(Merstone Junction-Ventnor West)

A hectic time at Merstone Junction Station in 1931. On the left of the picture, the preserved 'Terrier' tank No. 8 *Freshwater* (Which is now at Haven Street) stands with a train to Ventnor West. On the right, Drummond boilered '02' tank No. 27 *Merstone* departs for Sandown.

George H. Hunt

'Terrier' tank No. 12 *Ventnor* gently simmers in the station in the platform at Merstone Junction in 1929, before departing with a push-pull train to Ventnor West. The line from Merstone to St. Lawrence opened in 1897, and thence to Ventnor West in 1900. The line was worked by the Isle of Wight Central Railway from its opening until 1913, although it was a separate undertaking under the auspices of the Newport, Godshill and St. Lawrence Railway.

George H. Hunt

Godshill Station, pictured in 1932, was situated in the fields some way from the village. From Godshill, the line rose on gradients of 1:75 and 1:103.

George H. Hunt

Godshill Station by Jimmy James

Whitwell Station in 1927, when equipped with a passing loop and sidings.

George H. Hunt

Whitwell Station in 1933 with 'Terrier' tank No. 10 *Cowes* entering with a train for Ventnor West. By this time, the loop line had been removed and the up platform was left to the weeds.

George H. Hunt

Between Whitwell and St. Lawrence the line ran sharply downhill on a ledge high above the undercliff and the sea. This magnificent picture shows something of the splendid views that could be seen from the carriage window. 'Terrier' tank No. 11 *Newport*, now preserved at the Isle of Wight Steam Railway, propels a push-pull train towards St. Lawrence Tunnel.

George H. Hunt

St. Lawrence Station in 1933. The station was situated just at the southern end of St. Lawrence Tunnel.

George H. Hunt

A general view of Ventnor West Station in 1932. When the line was originally built, Ventnor West was called Ventnor Town. Ventnor West was situated behind the grounds of Steephill Castle.

George H. Hunt

One of the last two '02' tanks to be imported to the Isle of Wight, No. 35 *Freshwater*, soon after arrival at Ventnor West with a push-pull train from Merstone Junction.

John A. Britton

Ventnor West Station, 168 feet above sea level. Today the site has been built over with houses, although the station buildings remain.

John A. Britton

The exterior and station approach at Ventnor West. It was proposed, when the line was built, to continue it to a terminus near the Royal Hotel. Sadly the Ventnor West Branch closed in September 1952.

John A. Britton

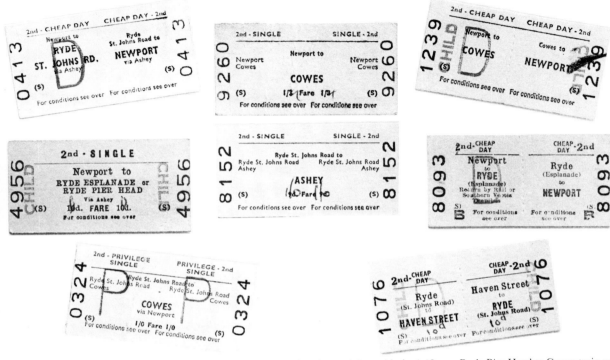

Driver Harold Lacey restarts No. 28 *Ashey* away from the original station at Ashey with the 1.18p.m. Ryde Pier Head to Cowes train on 30 December 1957. Originally, Ashey Station was provided with a passing loop, but it was taken out of use and converted to a long siding in 1926. The station served an adjacent racecourse which closed in 1929, although pony racing twice a year brought new life back to the station in latter years.

H. Peter Mason

No. 20 *Shanklin* leaves Ashey in July 1965. Serious subsidence under the original platform led the Southern Region of British Railways to re-align the track along the course of the old loop and erect a new platform and bus shelter type halt.

Dr Gerald R. Siviour

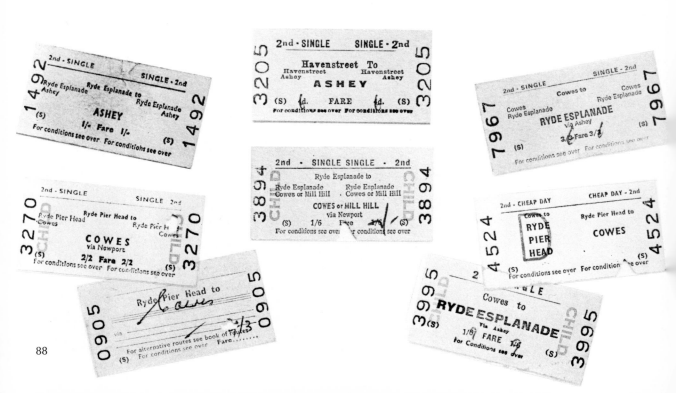

Ashey Station by Jimmy James

For many years the Isle of Wight stations competed for the title of 'Best Kept Station'. The competition was introduced by the Southern Railway and continued by British Railways Southern Region, being judged on station tidiness, and, where possible, the station garden. The annual competition winners were presented with a special station seat recording the winning stations. Porter-signalman Jess Wheeler of Haven Street stands beside the seat for the best kept station on 2 August 1958.

H. Peter Mason

A panoramic view of Haven Street Station taken from the top of a signal post. Haven Street was 5½ miles from Ryde Pier Head. This station was rebuilt in July 1926 with an island platform devoid of buildings. The station buildings were built alongside the up line at the top of a path leading down to the main road. The siding installed in 1886 for the Gas House, is pictured veering off to the left. By this time, however, the siding was only used for coal traffic and permanent way wagons.

H. Peter Mason

Token exchange at Haven Street from an on board approaching train. The 9.30 a.m. ex – Ryde train, hauled by the preserved No. 24 *Calbourne* on 31 August 1965. The signalman on the platform is Hughie White.

John Goss

Haven Street lever frame, 27 October 1957.

H. Peter Mason

Inside the station buildings was a sixteen lever signalling frame. Porter-signalman Jess Wheeler is pictured on 27 October 1957, shortly after accepting a train from Ryde!

H. Peter Mason

I wonder if this scene will ever be recreated by the Isle of Wight Steam Railway, which has its headquarters at Haven Street. Token exchange at Haven Street with the 2.28p.m. Ryde – Cowes train entering on 8 June 1957. Pictured on the platform is Signalman Jess Wheeler, and in the cab of engine No. 30 *Shorwell,* Fireman Brian Outley is ready to exchange tokens under the supervision of Driver George Ellis.

H. Peter Mason

A possible solution for unfortunate passengers who missed the last train of the day to Ryde! If they crossed Porter-signalman Terry Wright's hand with silver, they would get a lift in his BSA motorcycle and side car. Terry is pictured at Haven Street on 15 January 1966.

John Goss

Haven Street Station in 1932.

George H. Hunt

'The end of the line?' muses Gordon Pointer. Well not quite. He is in for a surprise.

Portsmouth and Sunderland Newspapers Ltd.,
Evening News

Signalman Jess Wheeler shouts a last minute message to Driver Nelson Parsons, on No. 17 *Seaview*, as he leaves Haven Street with the 11.31a.m. Cowes – Ryde Pier Head train on 11 March 1961.

H. Peter Mason

Gordon Pointer

I started work in early 1930, and like many other contemporaries, it was as a junior porter. I was at Newchurch Station. My wages were 16s per week. A junior porter in those days worked opposite turns to the grade one porter who was responsible for the station books and monthly accounts. When I reached the age of seventeen, my wages rose to £1 and increased by annual increments of 5s until I reached the age of twenty one. My second summer at Newchurch did not materialize, as I was moved to Wroxall on the Ryde – Ventnor main line for the summer, in order to allow Newchurch to be staffed by two adults. My summer at Wroxall was spent on the late turn every weekday and Sundays.

The following summer I was posted to Horringford. I recall one dark night, with the last train from Sandown to Newport after 10p.m., then the signalman from Merstone ringing me up. 'The fireman on that last train was not on the footplate when it arrived at Merstone,' said the Merstone signalman. Apparently the driver did not notice he was missing when he was not aboard to change over the staff and take the tablet for the Merstone – Shide section. I was instructed to start walking towards Merstone along the track, while the guard of the last train walked back towards me and Horringford Station. I naturally thought I would not see him alive again, but to my amazement I had not gone so far before I heard footsteps in the ballast coming towards me. It was him, dazed but all right! In those days, engines ran without doors or chains up in the cabs. Because of this incident all engines were provided with chains and strict instructions to be fastened at all times. Between Horringford and Merstone there happened to be a steep incline called Redway Bank, it was going up this that the fireman stepped outside to place a shovel on the outside rest, slipped and fell.

Very shortly after this unhappy event the Locomotive Inspector came over to see me from Eastleigh, Southampton. He informed me that the chap's brother who was also a fireman was killed in exactly the same way — by slipping from the footplate on a mainland Southern express engine.

Following a spell working at Ryde Pier and then as a shunter, I went to Merstone Junction as a grade one porter/signalman. This required me to attend the trains, act as booking clerk, and relieve the signalman between the early and late turns of duty. This was a very busy job and I was expected to work the 'Q freight' working, as guard between Merstone and Sandown daily.

I had a few years at Haven Street on the Newport – Ryde Line where my job was to work the signalbox, issue tickets to passengers (sometimes as much as 100 tickets to and from a train), and keep the station in tip top condition. On the platform, on many a winter's night I have struggled to relight the oil lamps, and have been glad to return to the box. A relief signalman told me one day before I was going on duty, that he detested working at Haven Street. He informed me that while he was having tea in the signalbox he heard a knocking at the window. It was an adder snake. (This was of course in the days before the porch was built when we had two privet hedges outside the signalbox door). After collecting the token from a train the relief signalman returned to find the snake inside the signalbox near the signal frame! I caught three myself one day and hung them on the fence at the back of the signalbox. It would be interesting to know if they come across any snakes nowadays at Haven Street Steam Railway.

While I was at Haven Street, each Tuesday one of the local farmers used to buy up heifer calves from Newport Market. He used to send off these calves; half a dozen at a time, to his brother in Herefordshire. We used to

Signalman Gordon Pointer at work inside Haven Street signalbox.

Betty Morley/Gordon Pointer Collection

A rare early view of Haven Street Station on 24 April 1927. Haven Street was unusual in having only foot crossing access to the island platform. Like many Isle of Wight stations, Haven Street was oil lit until closure.

Betty Morley/Gordon Pointer Collection

Off the catch points at Ryde St. John's Road. Driver Jim Stone and his locomotive, No. 25 *Godshill*, on 22 August 1957. Details of the accident are given on Page 95 by Signalman Gordon Pointer.

Eddie Prangnell

hold a certain early morning train in the platform at Haven Street until he had arrived. He used to roll in at the last minute, and I used to help him put the calves in sacks with their legs placed through holes in the sacks. I would hold the Newport and Cowes train because I didn't want half a dozen calves waiting and wandering around the signalbox.

The following year I went back to Merstone for a short time. One Sunday while catching the staff from a Sandown – Merstone train, we had an unfortunate mishap. The train was coming in so fast that the staff hit my thumb and bounced under the locomotive wheels. The staff was cut clean in half. Not being one to give up easily, I took the two halves back to the box where I could just turn the key section in the machine. This meant we could operate a train service for the rest of the day under the ticket system. The following day an official came out and it was pilot working between Merstone and Sandown for the next two weeks.

From here I went to Brading Box on the Ryde – Ventnor main line. This was a nice signalbox to work in, with plenty of mushrooms to pick from behind the bar for breakfast. It was not long before they moved me off to my final home – Ryde St. John's Road. I stayed here until I retired in November, 1978. This box had a bit of history surrounding it, as it was originally a South Eastern & Chatham Railway standard wooden signalbox from Waterloo Junction, and was brought over in 1928 to replace the old Ryde St. John's Road North and South boxes. We had forty levers with seven spares. The block sections were with Brading on the Ventnor Road, and Haven Street on the Cowes Road, but during the summer months the block section was with Smallbrook Junction.

If I was on the night turn at St. John's Road during the winter, one of the evening's highlights were the train 'races'. In theory this should never have happened, as the Ventnor and Cowes trains were booked at some minutes apart. The last trains of the night would wait for each other at St. John's Road, usually with Ken West as driver on one engine and Nelson Parsons on the other. They would wait for the off and away both trains would go to Smallbrook. On the return journey the two would race back from Cowes and Ventnor in order to be first to arrive at Ryde St. John's Road.

I remember one Sunday night heading off to Ryde St. John's very early, as the weather conditions were bad. In fact, my duty did not begin until 3a.m. Monday morning. Upon arriving at the box, I watched the last train from Ventnor with Ted Dale on the footplate put away the stock for the night in the siding. Presently, I heard the sound of trickling water under the box. Not long after that the river broke, and swamped the track bed between Smallbrook Junction and St. John's Road. The water poured over into the Works and Locomotive Shed filling the inspection pits and eventually rising to a considerable depth. The night staff at the Loco. Shed could not get a fire in any of the engines, as the bottom of the fireboxes were full of river flood water, with the consequence that the early morning mail trains could not run. At 6a.m. I

called for the governor, Mr Bert Smith, and told him to bring his wellington boots 'No, no,' he said. 'I won't need them.' He walked down with me to the station, and had to have a wooden plank laid from the platform into the box for him to walk on, as the water was so deep. We discovered that the ballast at Smallbrook had been completely washed away leaving the track in suspension some twelve feet above ground level. Ted Dale had certainly been very lucky! As I had arrived three hours early for work British Railways Southern Region awarded me a commendation and paid me for the extra three hours.

On another night I was sent down to Ryde Pier Head Signalbox for a turn of duty. I was working opposite turns to old Frank Smith, the relief signalman. We had a terrific storm on the Pier which shifted the down road. Two nights later there was another violent storm, at least Force 9! The box was rocking backwards and forwards, and the waves from the sea were pounding the sides. 'Well,' I thought. 'I'm not stopping here.' I walked down to the station and enquired what time high tide was. 'Not for another hour,' he replied. By the time I got back to the Pier Signalbox the sea had risen over the track, and cut it off. That was the worst I have ever seen it on Ryde Pier; the water was blowing fifty foot up in the air with that south-easterly gale!

The only accident I was involved with happened at St. John's Road Yard on 22 August 1957. Driver Jim Stone and his locomotive No. 25 *Godshill* came off the catch points while shunting. The shunter Mick Grist had the Annett's Key to work the ground frame, and upon giving a wrong instruction the locomotive moved forward with empty stock towards the main line. She went off on the catch points and over on her side in the brook. They came down to me at the box to report the incident, and it was decided to cover up the locomotive for the weekend until special equipment had arrived from Guildford. At the official enquiry at Woking, the shunter Mick Grist was let off all charges upon my assurance that he would never do anything like this again.

One thing I will never forget, was an incident when relieving at Ventnor Signalbox. It was the sight of Mad Jack Sturgess arriving from Ryde Pier Head Station and watering up his engine. 'Stop there, Bill. Leave the covers off. I'll water up the engine,' said Jack. So Bill Vallender, the driver, continued to oil up the front end of his engine. Meanwhile, the water filled in the tanks and gushed out over poor Bill soaking him. A typical Mad Jack Sturgess trick! After running round the train the driver wandered off into Ventnor Station to dry off his clothing, leaving Jack in charge of the locomotive. As soon as Bill had disappeared Mad Jack got out his telescope and peered up to the Downs. It wasn't long before a passenger standing on the platform asked, 'Why are you looking up there? What can you see?' Jack replied that he was looking at the cows on St. Boniface Down. These cows were rather special as to negotiate feeding on the slope, the cows needed two long legs and two short legs! You had to watch Mad Jack all the time.

Terry Wright

Today it is difficult to think that Haven Street Station — the home of the Isle of Wight Steam Railway Preservation Society — is that same station at which I served for so many years when it was under the ownership of British Railways. Yet, when I walk into the signalbox the memories come flooding back of these wonderful days when steamhauled trains to Ryde, Newport and Cowes were an everyday occurrence.

Following the closure in 1953 of Wootton and Whippingham stations and the down-grading of Ashey to a halt, Haven Street was the main station where trains could pass on the Newport – Ryde Line. In those days the station consisted of just an island platform with access via a foot crossing, which I believe was unique on the Island railways. The brick-built station building was constructed in 1926 and was separate from the platform. This accomodated a waiting room and combined signalbox/ booking office. Up until closure in February 1966 we had no gas or electricity, and oil lamps were the order of the day! The station sign on the exterior of the building was of interest to railway enthusiasts as it was slightly curved.

We took a tremendous pride in the appearance of our station and its gardens in those days. I am delighted to see that the volunteers today maintain the traditions of Hughie White and myself — they deserve that 'Best Kept Station' seat which is now in the museum at Haven Street.

During the winter season life could be very hard on your own out at Haven Street. One particular night in 1962 comes to mind. The last light engine movement of the night had passed off smoothly, with an engine from Newport to Ryde St. John's Road, when a blizzard began. The wind howled and the sky literally turned white, with the snow settling immediately. Returning to the signalbox, I attempted to pull the points to set the road for the 4a.m. mail train from Ryde Pier Head to Cowes, but the points would not move. I gathered up a shovel and set out to scrape away the snow from the point at the Ryde

end of the station over the road bridge. I then returned to the box and set this point in readiness for the mail train. The point at the Newport end of the station was a real problem. Although I cleared the snow away from it, by the time I returned to the signal box to pull the lever the snow had once more fallen to block it. I tried again to no avail! What could I do?

From my signalbox window, I could see a light on in the cottage of John Warn across the station yard. In desperation I decided to knock him up and ask for help. We arranged for him to wait in the box and pull the point lever when I signalled him in with a green light. At last success was achieved and the point was set. Little did I know that the mail train would not appear until late afternoon! Presently, Driver Jim Hunnybun walked through Haven Street along the track from Newport to Ryde as the roads were completely blocked. I, too, was unable to return to Ryde on my motorcycle and had to walk along the railway track into Ryde.

In *Once Upon A Line* Volume One, page 39, Driver Ken West mentions the tale of the cow which had its tail cut off by the 6.30p.m. from Cowes. What Ken didn't mention was that Relief Signalman George Abbott cleaned the cow's tail and hung it up outside Haven Street Signalbox with the label, 'The one that got away!' The sight of this attracted much interest from visiting railway enthusiasts who photographed it with glee.

One dark wet evening, I recall, a Medina Wharf – Ryde St. John's Road freight train was descending the 1:66 gradient from Briddlesford Copse. Goods trains in former times were required to stop at the distant signal and have their wagon brakes pinned down. However, this particular freight train had obviously failed to stop at the distant signal and was in trouble! It was due to pass a passenger train from Ryde at Haven Street which I had admitted into the section. The driver sounded the whistle at the distant signal, but kept on repeating six whistles all the way down. I decided to return to the signalbox and attempt to stop the train from Ryde by setting all the signals against it. Next, I opened the points for the freight train to pass straight through, so that the freight had more distance to pull up on the rising gradient of 1:70 at the Ashey end of the station. He managed to come to a halt just past the road bridge and quickly reversed back into the loop. The driver explained that the little '02' tank with sixteen loaded wagons behind just picked up speed and could not stop — had it been a Brighton 'E1' tank the problem would not have arisen!

On another occasion a freight train from Newport with twenty two empty wagons was due to pass straight through. If they were able to pass through Haven Street non-stop, the drivers would open up the engines as the curve into the loop could take trains up to 40m.p.h! Presently, I heard the sound of horses approaching under the road bridge. Curiousity caused me to wander up and see what was going on. Under the bridge was assembled the advance section of the local fox hunt. The next thing I knew was that one of the riders was attempting to open the gate to the station yard to cross the line. I walked across and warned them that a freight train was due through the station. The rider replied, in a plummy voice, that he had the right to cross the railway line whenever he pleased! After politely requesting several times that in the interests of safety the hunt should wait, I instructed him firmly to wait and suggested that the horses move back up the road in case they were alarmed by the noise of the train. Still he refused, with threats to report me to a higher authority if I did not let the hunt pass over the line! Within a minute the freight train thundered through and the engine's whistle must have frightened the horses. I looked round to meet the sight of bucking horses and swearing huntsmen displayed all over the ground.

One Sunday morning I remember sitting in the box reading the Sunday paper whilst waiting for the next train to pass through. It was such a nice morning, I decided to leave the door open and let the fresh air in. Engrossed in the football reports, I only slowly became aware of some movement in the room. Peering over the top of my paper, I was confronted by the head of a white swan looking over the top of the table. I decided to shoo it out, but to my surprise the swan hissed and set about me. Eventually I managed to grasp hold of the broom and drive him out. Immediately outside the entrance to the signalbox on the left was a five bar gate. I opened it in order to direct the swan though into the field at the back of the station. Roaming around the field was 'Noddy' a two ton steer. Thinking it was feeding time, seeing the gate open, Noddy made his way towards me. Meanwhile, the swan decided he would try to return inside the signalbox. It took quite a while and much chasing around to get the steer and the swan on the other side of the gate!

When trains were waiting to pass at Haven Street and perhaps one of them was late, the custom was for the driver to come into the box for a cup of tea with Hughie White or myself. On one such occasion Driver Tony Tiltman returned to his engine No. 26 *Whitwell*, which was deputising for his regular engine No. 24 *Calbourne*, and opened up the regulator of the engine. Suddenly there was a loud crack and the side rod fractured and dug into the ballast. Tony instinctively shut off steam and slammed on the brakes. Passengers on the 11.28a.m.

from Cowes to Ryde peered out of the carriage windows to see what had caused the abrupt halt. Such an occurrence could not have happened at a worse time for it was a July Saturday at 11.47a.m. — the peak of the summer season! I telephoned Ryde and arranged for a Southern Vectis bus to convey the stranded passengers into Ryde. Meanwhile, Tony Tiltman set about disconnecting *Whitwell's* fractured side rod. Luckily one of the passengers was none other than Ron Russell, the area inspector. He offered his assistance and enquired if he could be of any help to either Tony or myself. Seeing that everything was under control he volunteered to make teas for the passengers — a splendid public relations exercise! Eventually the whole train was towed into Ryde, with Tony gently opening the regulator to cushion *Whitwell's* cylinders. Within a week engine No. 26 *Whitwell* was fully repaired and back in service — a credit to the staff of Ryde Works.

During the night it was a common practice to have 'engineer's possession of the section of line' between Haven Street and Ryde or Haven Street and Newport. It was about 2a.m. one night and I had the kettle on ready for a brew to refresh the train crew on the ballast train from Newport. True to form the train pulled into the platform and stopped. Driver Roy Dyer and his fireman climbed down from their engine No. 27 *Merstone*, and made themselves at home in the signalbox, Five minutes passed and there was no sign of the guard, Jack Forrester. 'Has anyone seen Jack?' asked a Permanent Way ganger. Driver Dyer sent his fireman to search around for him. He returned to inform us that he had searched the yard, the toilets and looked in the large double verandah brake van, all to no avail! By now we were all getting a bit concerned and I collected a tilley lamp and set off up the end of the platform towards Wootton. Before I had gone a hundred yards, I noticed in the distance a flickering lamp approaching from under the bridge. We hailed Jack and enquired if he was all right. As we made our way back to the station, Jack explained that following the completion of ballasting at Whippingham, Roy Dyer had started No. 27 *Merstone* away so fast he had not had time to climb aboard his van — resulting in a long walk for Jack! 'I suppose they were thinking of your tea, Terry. I hope you saved a cup for me,' said the exhausted Jack Forrester.

Exchanging the single line token with trains passing straight through Haven Street was always a problem — especially if the drivers were making up lost time or if the fireman was young and inexperienced. I vividly remember the time a token exchange went wrong at Haven Street. An '02' tank engine entered the loop line bunker first towards Ryde with a late running freight to Ryde. The young fireman leaned out of the cab holding his hoop containing the single line token. As he approached at speed he lost confidence and dropped his token on the platform — but it did not land flat. Instead, the wire hoop coiled up like a spring with the speed it hit the ground and ricocheted off like a bullet, landing near the platelayer's hut. Meanwhile, the token for the Haven Street – Ryde section was successfully exchanged. Had that renegade token hit anyone they would have ended up in hospital.

We had excellent relations with neighbouring signalmen at Newport and Ryde (Smallbrook in the summer months). I remember one day receiving a telephone call from Signalman Ron Bennett at Newport, 'Look out on the next train for the Queen! Driver Ginger Minter has got the Royal Headcode on his engine No. 14!' Sure enough No. 14 *Fishbourne* pulled into the platform, complete with Royal Headcode, but unfortunately no Royalty aboard. On another occasion Ron telephoned me to say, 'Tell Guard Ron Childs that I might be getting on a bit, but I can tell the difference between a tail lamp and a red guard's hand lamp held in the rear window!' Apparently, Ron had climbed aboard his train at Newport and noticed

that he had forgotten to place the red tail lamp on the rear of the train. In fact, Signalman Bennett admired the quick improvisation of Guard Ron Childs — one of the best guards on the Isle of Wight railways.

During the last few weeks of operation we had many keen railway photographers visiting Haven Street taking pictures of the train. One afternoon one of these photographers asked permission to take pictures from the neighbouring field just up the line. I watched this fine gentleman as the afternoon freight roared up the bank with the smoke effects all laid on for the camera! At the crucial moment an inquisitive steer approached the photographer from the rear — what a picture that made!

Drummond boilered '02' tank No. 31 *Chale* with Driver Cyril Eason at the regulator, roars up through the cutting towards Wootton Station.

R. J. Blenkinsop

The former single platform station at Wootton sadly closed in 1953. This station was unusual in that its offices were accommodated in an arch of the road overbridge. A siding was located on the other side of the bridge which was mainly used for local coal traffic. Due to earth slips, the station and cutting were filled in for safety reasons, but a new station is under construction on the other side of the bridge.

George H. Hunt

Wootton Station by Jimmy James

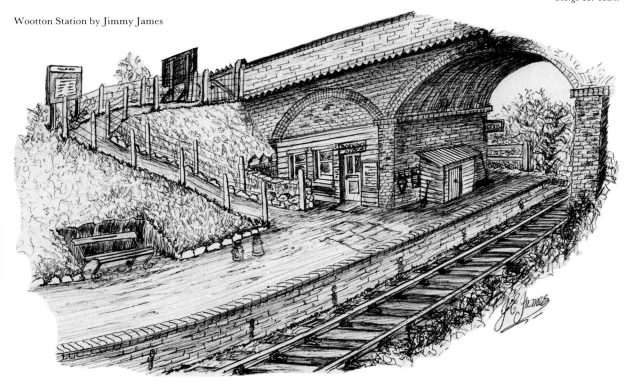

Whippingham Station in 1933. Engine No. 28 *Ashey* with a Drummond Boiler is about to depart with a train for Ryde Pier Head. Driver Harold Lacey can be seen looking out of his cab on the left hand side. By this time the station was open to the general public, but the appearance of the station and its gardens were maintained almost to the standard of Queen Victoria's era.

George H. Hunt

Whippingham Station staff. Signa
Lewis, Ben Steadman and Jim Hoope
Jim Hooper Col

An extraordinary view of Newport Station as seen from the top of the Gas Works. The up 11.31a.m. Cowes – Ryde Pier Head train is leaving Newport on 27 May 1958. There is so much detail in this picture: Newport 'A' Signalbox, a carriage set being cleaned and oiled, and a train preparing to depart for Cowes from the down platform.

H. Peter Mason

"DID YOU SEE HIM JUMP!"

Mad Jack Sturgess

They called him Mad Jack as he raced down the track,
Devising the wildest of schemes.
'A practical joker,' claims Roy, his ex-stoker;
His tricks were more nightmares than dreams.

His loco, elite of a railway so neat,
Distinct by its smokebox 'Brass star',
Brings memories fading of No. 22 *Brading*
So vividly back from afar.

Not only his jesting, but trains alway testing,
He raced them from Ryde to Smallbrook,
With Roy at the fire, the pressure rose higher,
At Apse Bank the challenge Jack took.

He courted disaster by driving trains faster,
But one night he answered the call,
When he sprinted the track, for to hold a train back,
Saving lives by the score at Wroxall.

He relaxed with a book, a good swim or fish hook,
At Ryde Pier he'd often be met,
And the stories now told, by his friends growing old,
Are legends we should not forget.

Joan M. Britton

Isle of Wight Central Railway Working Time Table, October 1909.

Oct 1909

I.W. of Wight Central Railway.

WORKING TIME TABLE

FOR

October, 1 __, nd until further n __es.

PRIVATE

For the information of the Company's Servants only.

General Offices,
Newport, I.W.

CHAS. L. CONACHER
General Manager.

RYDE LINE.

UP.

Miles			1 Mail En a.m.	2 Mail En a.m.	3 Mixed a.m.	4 Pass. a.m.	5 Mixed a.m.	6 Lt. En noon	7 Pass	8 Mxd p.m.	9 Pass p.m.	10 Pass p.m.	11 Lt.En p.m.	12 Mixed p.m.	13 Mail p.m.	14 Pass	1 Mail.En a.m.	2 Pass a.m.	3 Goods noon	4 Pass p.m.	5 Mixed p.m.	6 Pass p.m.
	NEWPORT	dep	2 30		7 25	9 25	10 25		1 10	1 10	5 0	5 45		8 0	8 45		10 15	12 0	2 40	4 25	8 20
2¼	Whippingham	A			7 30	9 31	10 31	—	1 15	1 15	5 5	5ps49		8 6	8ps49		10 20	12—7	2 45	4 30	8 25
3½	Wootton	A			7 33	9 34	10 34	—	1 18	1 18	5 8	5 52		8 10	8A51		10 23	12—10	2 48	4 33	8 27
4½	Haven Street	A	2 45		7 38	9 40	10 39	—	1 24	1 22	5 12	5ps55		8 16	8ps54		10 28	12—16	2 51	4 39	8 32
6	Ashey	A			7 43	9 43	10B44		1 28	1 26	5 16	5ps58		8E22	8ps57		10 32	12—22	2 54	4 44	8 37
8¼	Ryde (St. John's Rd) arr				7 48	9 48	10 50		1 33	1 32	5 22	6 C3		8 29	9 3	9 40	10 39	12 30	2 59	4 50	8 43
8½	Ryde (St. John's Rd) dep		2 55	2 30		9 49	10 51	12 10	1 34		5 23	6	7 55	8 30	9 4		10 40	12 45	3 1	4 51	8 45
9	Ryde (Esplanade) dep		2 58	2 33		9 52	10 53	12 13	1 37		5 27	6	7 58	8 32	9 7		10 43	12 48	3 4	4 53	8 47
9½	RYDE (Pier Head) arr		3 0	2 35		9 55	10 55	12 15	1 40		5 30	6	8	8 35	9 10		10 45	12 51	3 5	4 55	8 50

A Calls by Signal. B Cross No. 3 Down. C Cross No. 8 Down. E Cross No. 10 Down.

NOTES. Week-days.—No. 3 Must run to time to prevent delay to London Services.
Nos. 5, 7 & 12. Not more than one spring buffered wagon, with screw coupling must be attached to these Trains without special authority. No intermediate Sidings to be worked unless ordered.
No. 14 Cross No. 11 Down at Ashey.

Ryde Goods Trains to run as per notice between 6 a.m. and 7 a.m.

NOTES —Sundays—
No. 6 to convey Mails, Vans to be left at Pier Head.

ELECTRIC BLOCK. Newport, Wootton, Ashey. TELEPHONE, Newport, Whippingham, Wootton, Haven Street, Ashey, Ryde.

DOWN.

Miles		1 Mail a.m.	2 Pass a.m.	3 Pass. a.m.	4 Lt.En a.m.	5 Mixed noon	6 Pass p.m.	7 Pass. p.m.	8 Pass. p.m.	9 Lt.En p.m.	10 Pass p.m.	11 Emp. p.m.	12 Mail En. p.m.	13 Pass. p.m.	1 Mail a.m.	2 Pass a.m.	3 Mixed p.m.	4 Pass. p.m.	5 Mixed p.m.	6 Pass. p.m.
	RYDE (Pier Head) dep	3 25	8 20	10 30	11 5	12 20	3 35	3 50	6 0	6 25	8	8 35	9 20		3 25	10 50	1 15	3 10	6 20	8 55
	Ryde (Esplanade) dep	3 30	8 22	10 32	11 7	12 22	2 37	3 52	6 2	6 27	8 7	8 37	9 22		3 30	10 52	1 17	3 12	6 22	8 57
1¼	Ryde (St. John's Rd) arr	3 33	8 24	10 34	11 10	12 21	2 39	3 54	6 5	6 30	8 9	8 40	9 25		3 33	10 54	1 19	3 14	6 25	8 59
1½	Ryde (St. John's Rd) dep	3D35	8 30	10 37		12 30	2 44	3 59	6C10		8 14	9 30	9 45		3D35	10 57	1 22	3 18	6 28	9 5
3½	Ashey	A	3E43	8 38	10B44		12 38	2 50	4 5	6 18		8 22	9 40	9 52		3E43	11 4	1 29	3 24	6 35	9 12
5	Haven Street	A	pass	8 42	10 48		12 42	2 54	4 9	6 22		8 26	9 45	9 56		pass	11 7	1 33	3 28	6 38	9 15
6½	Wootton	dep	pass	8 46	10 53		12 47	2 58	4 13	6 27		8 31	9 55	10A1		pass	11 12	1 38	3 32	6 44	9 20
7½	Whippingham	A	3F55	8 49	10 55		12 50	3 0	4 15	6 30		8 34	10 0	10 4		3F55	11 14	1 40	3 34	6 47	9 23
9½	NEWPORT	arr	4 0	8 55	11 0		12 55	3 5	4 20	6 35		8 40	10 10	10 10		4 0	11 20	1 45	3 39	6 53	9 28

A. Calls by Signal. B. Cross No 5 Up unless late. C. Cross No. 10 Up at St. John's Road. G. Cross No. 12 Up.

NOTES. Week-days.
No. 11 cross No. 14 Up at Ashey.
No. 1 D—Arrive on I.W.R. Road, cross over and pick up Tablet. E—Tablet and Staff. F—Stop for Bridge Test.

NOTES. Sundays.
No. 3. Train Coaches of No. 12 Up, Saturdays, to be left at St. John's Road for this working. and cleaned there

STAFF SECTION. Newport to Ashey. ELECTRIC TABLET. Ashey to Ryde (St. John's Road).

VENTNOR LINE.

DOWN.

Miles			1 Goods a.m.	2 Mixed a.m.	3 Pass. a.m.	4 Pass noon	5 Pass. p.m.	6 Exprs p.m.	7 Pass p.m.	8 Mixed p.m.	9 Pass p.m.	1 Mixed a.m.	2 Pass p.m.
	MERSTONE Jct.	dep	7 0	9 18	10 32	12 10	1 20	pass	5 35	8 15	9 24	9 30	8 34
1½	Godshill	A dep	7 15	9 22	10 36	12 13	1 25	4 5	5 39	8 19	9 28	9 35	8 39
4	Whitwell	,	7 45	9 29	10 41	12 18	1 31	4A9	5 45	8 24	9 33	9 40	8 45
5½	St. Lawrence	A ,	7 55	9 35	10 45	12 22	1 35	4A12	5 50	8 31	9 37	9 45	8 50
6½	VENTNOR Town	arr	8 5	9 40	10 50	12 25	1 40	4 15	5 55	8 35	9 40	9 50	8 55

A. Stops by Signal.

N.B. All Passenger Trains must stop momentarily outside Ventnor Home Signals—Goods Trains to stop dead.

NOTES. Week-days.
No. 1 Take all Ventnor Line Wagons Must work to time. Shunt Ventnor Yard on arrival. Load Sand | N.B.—See Main Line Sheet for Branch Engine Working.
when required. No. 3, 4, 6, & 8 Through Trains Cowes to Ventnor Town.
ELECTRIC BLOCK. Merstone Junction, Godshill, Whitwell, Ventnor Town
TELEPHONE. Same, including St. Lawrence.

UP.

Miles			1 Mixed a.m.	2 Pass. a.m.	3 Pass. a.m.	4 Pass. noon	5 Pass p.m.	6 Pass. p.m.	7 Pass p.m.	8 Pass p.m.	9 Pass p.m.	1 Mixed a.m.	2 Pass p.m.
	VENTNOR Town	dep	8 25	9 45	10 55	12 30	2 45	4 45	6 4	8 40	9 45	10 35	9 0
1¼	St. Lawrence	A	8 30	9 50	10 59	12 34	2 39	4 49	6 4	8 44	9 49	10 39	9 4
2½	Whitwell	dep.	8 35	9 55	11 3	12 38	2 43	4 53	6 8	8 48	9 53	10 44	9 8
5	Godshill	A	8 40	9 59	11 7	12 42	2 47	4 57	6 12	8 52	9 57	10 48	9 12
6½	MERSTONE Jct.	arr.	8 45	10 4	11 10	12 50	2 52	4 59	6 15	8 55	10 0	10 52	9 15

NOTES.—Week-days. A Calls by Signal.
No. 1 to bring all Ventnor Line Wagons Heavy Engine. Must run to time.
No. 3 4. & 6 Must run to time. Through Trains to Cowes.
STAFF SECTION. Merstone Junction to Whitwell. Whitwell to Ventnor Town.

N.B.—Every effort must be made to work the Branch Trains to time, so that delay may not result to the Main Line Trains.

SANDOWN LINE.

DOWN.

		1	2	3	4	5	6	7	8	9	10	11	12	13	14	15	16		1	2	3	4	5	6
		WEEK-DAYS.																	**SUNDAYS.**					
Miles		Goods a.m.	Goods a.m.	Mxd a.m.	Mxd a.m.	Pass. a.m.	Goods a.m.	Pass	Pas p m	Goods	Pas p m	Exp	Pass p m	Pas p m	Mxd	Goods	Pass		Goods a.m.	Mixed a.m.	Pass p.m.	Mxd p.m.	Goods p.m.	Pass p m
NEWPORT	dep	6 30	6 45	7 40	9 0	10 20		12 0 noon	1 5		3 10	3 50	5 15	5 20	8 0	8 30		9 10	8 50	9 17	12 55	2 50	5 15	8 20
Pan Lane Siding	"	pass	7 0	7A44	9A 8	10A23			1A9		3,14	pass		5A23	8A 4			9 14	9 5	9A21	12A59	2A 54		8A24
Shide	dep	pass		7 47	9 12	10 26	B		1 12		3 17	pass		5 26	8 8			9 17	pass	9 24	1 3	2 58		8 27
Blackwater			6 50	7 51	9 16	10 30		12 9	1 17		3 21	4p50		5 30	8 12	8 45		9 22	9 15	9 28	1 7	3 2	5 30	8 31
MERSTONE Junct.	arr			7 53	9 18	10 32	11 15	12 10	1 20		3 23		5 25	5 32	8 15	9 15		9 24	9 24	1 9	3 4	5 45		8 33
MERSTONE Junct	dep			7 57	9 22	10 36	11 20	12 14	1 24		3 27			5 36	8 19			9 26	9 34	1 13	3 8			8 38
Horringford	A			8 1	9 26	10 40		12 17	1 27		3 30			5 40	8 22			9 28	9 37	1 16	3 10			8 41
Newchurch	A			8 5	9 30	10 44		12 20	1 30		3 34			5 44	8 25			9 31	9 40	1 20	3 14			8 45
Alverstone	A			8 7	9 32	10 46		12 22	1 32		3 36			5 46	8 27			9 36	9 42	1 22	3 16			8 48
SANDOWN	arr.			8 10	9 38	10 48		12 25	1 35		3 38			5 48	8 30	9 45		9 40	9 45	1 25	3 20	6 15		8 50

A Stops by Signal. **N.B. Engines must not run coupled between Newport and Merstone Junction.** **N.B.—The maintenance of connection with I.W.R. Trains is of first importance**

NOTES. Week-days. B.—Branch Engine work Horringford Pit if necessary.
No. 1 Take all Ventnor Line Wagons. Load sand as required.
No. 2 Engine of 7-25 Newport to Ryde. Work Pan and Shide to relieve Ventnor Goods.
No. 3. Convey Mew's and Crouchers Sandown Traffic. No. 7 must run to time. Work through to Ventnor.

SUNDAYS.
No. 1 take empty Vectis Wagons to Shide Pit.
No. 5 leave on arrival of No. 1 Up. Worked by 3-45 p.m. Freshwater Engine.

ELECTRIC TABLET—Newport, Shide, and Merstone. ELECTRIC BLOCK—Merstone, Newchurch, and Sandown.
TELEPHONE.—All Stations.

UP.

		1	2	3	4	5	6	7	8	9	10	11	12	13	14	15	16		1	2	3	4	5	6	7
		WEEK-DAYS.																	**SUNDAYS**						
Miles		Goods a.m.	Pass	Mixed a.m.	Pass a.m.	Goods a.m.	Pass p.m.	Goods	Mxd p.m.	Eng. p.m.	Pass p m	Pass p m	Pass p m	Pass	Gds	Pass	Goods	Goods	Mixed	Goods	Pass	Mixed	Goods	Pass p.m.	Good
SANDOWN	dep		8 30	9 45	10 55		12 30		2 35	3 55		6 08	8 40		9 45		10 0	10 35		2 15	4 40	6 30	9 0	
Alverstone	A		8 34	pass	10 59		12 34		2 39	3 59		6 4	8 44		9 49			10 39		2 18	4 44		9 4	
Newchurch	A		8 37		11 2		12 37		2 42	4 2		6 8	8 47		9 52			10 43		2 21	4 47		9 7	
Horringford	A		8 41		11 5	11 35	12 40		2 45	4 6		6 12	8 51		9 56			10 46		2 24	4 50		9 11	
MERSTONE Junct.	arr		8 45	10 3	11 9	11 40	12 45		2 50	4 10		6 17	8 55		10 0			10 50		2 28	4 54		9 15	
MERSTONE Junct	dep		8 47	10 5	11 12		12 47		2 52	4 12	3 0	6 19	8 58	9 15	10 3		10 30	10 54	11 5	2 33	4 57	7 0	9 17	9 30
Blackwater	A		8 51	pass	11 16		12 53		2 57	4 17		6 23	9 2					10 59	11 10	2 36	5 2		9 21	
Shide	dep	7 10	8A54	pass	11A20		12A55		3A1	5A7		6A26	9A6		10A18		A	11A1	11A20	2A34	5A5		9A24	
NEWPORT	arr	7 15	8 58	10 15	11 24		1 0		3 5	3 10	4 25	5 18	6 30	9 10	9 30	10 15	10 45	10 30	11 5	11 25	2 37	5 8		9 28	9 45

A Stops by Signal. N.B.—Engines must not run coupled between Newport and Merstone Junction.

NOTES Week-days. No. 3 Must run to time. Attach Wagons of No. 1 Up Branch at Merstone. No. 5 ex Horringford Pit
if necessary. No. 6 must not be held at Sandown after 12-35 p.m. and work to Merstone only.
No. 14 Return of 8-30 p.m. Goods from Newport.

SUNDAYS.
No. 2 To clear out Shide and take up working of 12-0 noon Ryde Goods.
No. 5 Engine to work No. 2 Down Branch.

TABLET SECTIONS. Newport, Shide, and Merstone. STAFF SECTION. Merstone Junction to Sandown.

COWES LINE.

DOWN.

		1	2	3	4	5	6	7	8	9	10	11	12		1	2	3	4	5	6	7
		WEEK-DAYS.													**SUNDAYS.**						
Miles		Mail a.m.	Mixed a.m.	Pass. a.m.	Pass. a.m.	Pass. a.m.	Pass. p.m.	Pass. p.m.	Pass. p.m.	Pass. p.m.	Pass. p.m.	Pass. p.m.	Pass. p.m.		Mail a.m.	Pass. a.m.	Pass. a.m.	Pass. p.m.	Pass. p.m.	Pass. p.m.	Pass. p.m.
NEWPORT	dep	5 10	8 15	9 5	11 5	11 26	1 5	3 10	4 30	5 15	6 40	8 0	9 15		5 10	9 35	11 25	2 0	3 42	5 10	9 30
Cement Mills	B		8 19	9 9		11 29		3 13	4 34		6 44		9 19			9 39	11 27	2 3	3 45	5 14	9 34
Medina Wharf	pass	5 19	8 23	9 13	11 11	11 33	1 13	3 17	4 39	5 22	6 47	8 8	9 23		5 19	9 43	11 32	2 6	3 49	5 18	9 38
Mill Hill	dep		8 28	9 18		11 38	1 18	3 21	4 43	5 26	6 53	8 12	9 27			9 48	11 37	2 11	3 53	5 23	9 43
COWES	arr.	5 25	8 30	9 20	11 15	11 40	1 20	3 25	4 45	5 28	6 55	8 15	9 30		5 25	9 50	11 40	2 13	3 55	5 25	9 45

Wharf Engine to work as required. N.B.—No Trains must cross at Medina Wharf in either direction. No. 1 to be worked by Wharf Engine. Must reach Cowes
by 5-30 a.m. No. 5, 6, & 9 Week-days, must run to time. No. 6 not cal. at Mills.
ELECTRIC TABLET. Newport, Medina Wharf, Cowes. TELEPHONE. Newport, Cement Mills, Wharf Box, Medina Wharf, Mill Hill, Cowes.

UP.

		1	2	3	4	5	6	7	8	9	10	11	12	13		1	2	3	4	5	6
		WEEK-DAYS.														**SUNDAYS.**					
Miles		Pass. a.m.	Pass. a.m.	Pass. a.m.	Pass. p.m.	Pass. p.m.	Exprs p.m.	Pass. p.m.	Pass. p.m.	Goods p.m.	Mixed p.m.	Mail p.m.	Pass. p.m.	Pass		Pass. a.m.	Pass. p.m.	Pass p.m.	Pass p.m.	Pass p.m.	Pass p.m.
COWES	dep	8 45	10 0	11 45	12 40	2 50	3 35	5 5	5 31		7 40	8 30	9 45	10 0		10 0	12 40	2 20	4 5	5	10 0
Mill Hill		8 47	10 2	11B47	12 42	2 52	3B37	5A7	5 33		7 42	8B32	9 47	10 2		10 2	12 42	2 22	4 7	5 7	10 2
Medina Wharf	pass	8 51	10 7	11 49	12 47	2 57	3 41	5 13	5 36	6 0	7 46	8 36	9 52	10 7		10 6	12 46	2 26	4 12	8 10	10 7
Cement Mills	A	8 54	10 11		12 51	3 0			5 40	6 15	7 49		9 56	10 11		10 9	12 49	2 30	4 16	8 13	10 11
NEWPORT	arr	8 58	10 15	11 56	12 55	3 5	3 47	5 15	5 43	6 30	7 55	8 42	10 0	10 15		10 13	12 53	2 34	4 20	8 17	10 15

No. 4. must run to time. **N.B.—No Trains must cross at Medina Wharf in either direction.**

A. Saturdays only and other days at Station Master's discretion. No. 9. shunting Engine from Wharf,
clear Mills. B. Calls by signal. No. 13 must connect with Southampton Boat.

N.B. Wharf Engine to work as required.

FRESHWATER LINE.

DOWN.

		1	2	3	4	5	6	7	8		1	2	3
		WEEK-DAYS.									**SUNDAYS.**		
Miles		Mail & Goods a.m.	Pass. a.m.	Mixed a.m.	Pass p.m.	Pass p.m.	Mixed p.m.	Pass p.m.	Pass p.m.		Mail a.m.	Mixed a.m.	Pass
NEWPORT	dep	4 30	9 2	11 30	1 10	3 15	4 35	6 40	9 15		4 30	11 35	7 0
Carisbrooke	dep	—	9 9	11A37	1 17	3A22	4 48	6 47	9A22			11A42	7 7
Watchingwell	A		9 14	11 42	1 23		4 53	6 52	9 28			11 49	7 14
Calbourne	dep	4 50	9 19	11A47	1A27	3A32	4 58	6A56	9 33		4 50	11A52	7 17
Ningwood	dep	5 5	9 23	11A52	1A32	3A37	5 4	7A1	9 37		5 5	11A55	7 21
Yarmouth	dep	5 30	9 32	12 0	1 40	3 45	5 10	7 10	9 45		5 30	12 5	7 30
FRESHWATER	arr	5 40	9 37	12 5	1 45	3 50	5 15	7 15	9 55		5 40	12 10	7 35

A Calls by signal.

NOTES.—Weekdays. No. 1 Take forward all Goods traffic. Unload Mails and shunt at Yarmouth as required.
Must reach Freshwater by 5-45 a.m. Shunt at Freshwater and return with 8-15 a.m. train. No. 2 must work
to time. No. 3. To convey none but urgent Wagons. No. 5 must work to time. Stop at Watchingwell for
Tenants only. No. 6 Cross No. 5 Up at Carisbrooke. Train to be left at Freshwater for 8-15 a.m. working

SUNDAYS.
No. 1 convey Mails only. Return with No. 1 Up.

ELECTRIC BLOCK. Carisbrooke, Calbourne, Ningwood, Yarmouth and Freshwater. TELEPHONE. Same.

UP.

		1	2	3	4	5	6	7	8	9		1	2	3
		WEEK-DAYS.										**SUNDAYS.**		
Miles		Mixed a.m.	Pass a.m.	Mixed noon	Pass p.m.	Mxd. p.m.	Goods p.m.	Pass p.m.	Pass p.m.	Mixed p.m.		Pass. a.m.	Pass. p.m.	Pass p.m.
FRESHWATER	dep	8 15	9 42	12 20	2 25	4 20	5 45	6 15	7 20	10 0		8 40	3 45	7 40
Yarmouth	dep	8 20	9 47	12 25	2 30	4 25	5 50	6 5	7 25	10 5		8 45	3 50	7 45
Ningwood	dep	8A30	9 55	12 33	2 38	4 33	6 13	6 11	7A33	10A14		8 53	3 58	7 53
Calbourne	dep	8A35	10 0	12 38	2A43	4 38		6 17	7A38	10A18		8 58	4 2	7 58
Watchingwell	A	8 42	10 4	12 42	2 47	4 42	6 20	6 21	7 42	10A22		9 2	4 8	8 1
Carisbrooke	dep	8 50	10 10	12 48	2A53	4 48	6 28	6A27	7A48	10A28		9 8	4 12	8 8
NEWPORT	arr	8 55	10 17	12 55	3 0	4 55	6 35	6 37	7 55	10 35		9 14	4 20	8 15

A Calls by signal.

NOTES. Weekdays.
No. 2 must run to time.
No. 6 Goods Train except Saturdays. Cross No. 7 Down at Carisbrooke when work requires.

SUNDAYS.
No. 2 Engine to work Sandown Goods

STAFF SECTIONS. Newport to Carisbrooke. Carisbrooke to Ningwood. Ningwood to Freshwater.

General Note. — The times of Goods Trains are fixed to give the latest running allowed. Earlier running is not prohibited if line clear.

R. W. Kemp FCIT

I worked for a short period of time at the Isle of Wight Central Railway offices between 1911 and 1916. The staff in the head offices of the Company comprised the general manager, the secretary and the accountant's department. The total staff numbered about twenty.

The first typewriter was installed in 1911; but it was some little while afterwards the practice ceased of writing in copying ink, and making copies in the tissue copying book using hand presses. The first duplicator was a 'Plex' which was a slate coloured claylike material contained in a rectangular tin. Copies were taken from a master hand-written paper by rubbing the master sheet and afterwards each separate sheet of paper by hand, on to the surface of the clay. One of the regular uses of this duplicator for the Central Railway was the production of a return, in common with the other UK railways, showing the weekly gross receipts. This was used on the London Stock Exchange in assessing the value of the railway's shares and dividend prospects.

The duplicating machine could cause problems in the Isle of Wight Central office by accident or carelessness. I recall when a junior clerk had a small bottle of indelible ink knocked out of his hand on to the carpet of the general manager, Mr Russell Willmott. This was not the end of the matter, for he left his mark on the door handle of the Chief's door and the Chief had the unpleasant and irritating task of getting the stains from his hands! Suffice it to say that the junior was barred from entry into that particular room with such a dangerous object.

Russell Willmott, our general manager, although a very strict disciplinarian, as was paramount in those days, was very mindful of the welfare of his staff. He will be remembered by many for a number of outings he gave to Sandown in the saloon coach in the summer, for cricket matches and swimming followed by high tea. In the winter, he ran a train and boat trip to Portsmouth for a theatre matinee followed by tea. I always will remember the thrill given to the boys on the railway when Mr Willmott gave permission for several hours absence (unsolicited) to leave and walk up to Albany Barracks at Parkhurst, to watch the Trooping of the Colours by the Royal Fusiliers in their scarlet uniforms and busbies.

Such treats were bound to linger in our memories when one received something like five shillings a week for boy clerks, and not much more for the juniors who would not consider themselves boys. There were no ladies in the Central Railway offices until the 1914-18 War meant the departure and loss of able bodied members of the office.

There was a daily time signal sent out to all stations from Newport; about twenty were given by pre-arrangement. It was a standing instruction that at each station the stationmaster or booking clerk would be available at the Company's telephone at 10 a.m. each day. Then at the appointed hour the telephone instruments at the head office would be operated by the junior staff.

During the winter when cash takings at some remote village stations were negligible it was observed that the cash remittance statement which accompanied the cash takings (conveyed to Newport Office in the leather bag by the first train each morning) were for a particular station confined to a few pence. They were itemed under the heading 'lavatory receipts', eventually suspicion was aroused that the stationmaster concerned was very loath to send in a nil return, and saw to it that a few pence at least should be remitted in favour of his quiet days.

During this period it is of interest to note that the station mistresses at Alverstone, Whippingham and Watchingwell operated all duties single handed. They competently undertook ticket work, parcel work and all clerical work. I admired them tremendously.

Many of the Isle of Wight Central Railway personalities came from Warwickshire, and were closely connected with the Stratford-on-Avon & Midland Junction Railway. Lord Willoughby de Broke who was a Director of the Isle of Wight Central Railway lived at Warwick Castle, and Russell Willmott, the general manager and company secretary originally lived in Avenue Road, Leamington Spa. H. Willmott was the company chair-

A period piece! Newport Station staff in 1895. In its heyday, Newport Station could justifiably be called the 'Clapham Junction' of the Isle of Wight.

Dr John Mackett Collection

Newport Station staff in 1910. Newport was 10 miles from Ryde Pier Head and the station buildings included the offices and head-quarters of the Isle of Wight Central Railway Company. The station was situated north of the town centre on a bank to the west side of the River Medina.

Timothy P. Cooper Collection

The Isle of Wight Central Railway General Strike of September 1919. The picture shows a mass meeting of IWCR staff outside the Guildhall at Newport.

Timothy P. Cooper Collection

man, also from Leamington Spa, and his companions G. R. Newcombe, the assistant general manager, and W. J. Sawkins, the accountant, came down to the Isle of Wight Central Railway from Warwickshire. In 1913, of course, it was Russell Willmott, the general manager, who revolutionised the Island railways by being the first to introduce Third Class travel on all Isle of Wight Central trains.

W. A. 'Bill' Barton

Born in 1904, I started work with the Isle of Wight Central Railway managed by the Willmott family, at the age of fourteeen years in December 1918. Four months later in April 1919 I became a bound apprentice with working hours from 7.30a.m. until 5p.m. during the week, and 7.30a.m. until 1p.m. on Saturdays. All for the enormous wage of 6 shillings a week. There was an annual rise of 1 shilling a week until 1921. The Willmotts were very strict with time keeping, and such things as breaking or losing a tool or wasting electricity. We would get fined or a day or two suspension. Smoking at work was forbidden on the Isle of Wight Central Railway in those days and would result in a hefty fine if caught, and a note would be entered on your record card. Things were so strict that if we had to replace lost or broken tools, then we would have to visit Morgans the local ironmonger.

The depot was at Newport and my home was only five minutes' walk away. It was not long before I teamed up with a telegraph lineman, and the work entailed box signalling Intermediate 'Tablet Instruments', Preeces, Wire Blocks, station lighting and Medina Wharf work. Saturday mornings were set aside for attending the eight electric motors driving machinery in the Isle of Wight Central workshops, and pumping water from a well for locomotives. Only very occasionally did we wander into the running shed to check the carbon filament lamps, as they lasted well.

In 1921, I had an increase of 3 shillings a week, and shortly afterwards found myself without a lineman (as he emigrated). I therefore took over the district before my apprenticeship had completed its term. Two years later the Southern Railway took over and I came under Eastleigh. Suddenly my district on the Islands railways stretched from thirty miles to sixty miles and I found myself promoted to chief lineman with a staff of six. The old Freshwater, Yarmouth & Newport Railway section was in a state of shambles — the previous maintenance was carried out by one of their platelayers. Single Needle Telegraph instruments had to be replaced with magnetic telephones and the highway crossing gates were connected with a warning system. This had an immediate effect — there were fewer crossing gates smashed!

On the Ryde – Ventnor and Brading – Bembridge Branch sections I replaced Telegraph Instruments, and Webb-Thompson Staff Instruments were installed at Wroxall along with magnetic telephones. Slowly, with the help of gangs sent over from Eastleigh on the mainland, I managed to replace all the ancient lower quadrant signals with their wooden posts. The tall spiked finials and wooden signal arms gave way to the Southern's South Western style signals, with lattice posts and corrugated or flat metal arms. Later on, a telephone exchange was installed at Newport, and all circuits were converted from 'earth-return' to 'metallic'.

With the various cutbacks, I abolished a number of signal boxes: Ventnor West, Ashey, Whippingham and St. John's Road North. Following the closure of Whitwell Box, I purchased it for three pounds and this is now resurrected in the garden as a useful shed.

While the signalbox at Ashey was in existence after the closure, it was opened twice a year for the Ashey Races. The ten lever frame was used to berth four or five trains up in the siding at the back of the stand. I used to send out a signalman called Harry Matthews from Newport North to man the box. It was two days at the races for me however!

I remember one morning installing some warning bells just outside St. Lawrence Tunnel on the Ventnor West Line, for the public crossing. The bells were worked by a mercury treadle. As I was finishing I heard some gun shots, and wondered what was going on. They continued at regular intervals, and so I walked up to the station, and discovered the stationmaster, Mr Phil Corrick, shooting at something from the platform on to the cliff. 'That's my dinner,' he said. Apparently, he was shooting at rabbits, hoping they would roll down the cliff, but he had little success that day.

If I had half an hour to kill at Newport, I liked to go down for a cup of tea with signalman Jim Hooper at Newport South Box. This was the signalbox that controlled the Medina Drawbridge. I remember the day when a Mew Langton Brewery barge got stuck, obstructing the closure of the bridge. Len Creeth, who was in charge of maintenance of the bridge, had a few heated words with the captain of the boat at the time.

After the amalgamation of the Island's railways under the Southern Railway in 1923, there were still two separate tracks from Ryde to Smallbrook. One track carried the former Isle of Wight Central line towards Newport and Cowes, the other carried the former Isle of Wight Railway line towards Brading and Ventnor. There was no connection between the two roads until 1926, when owing to increasing holiday traffic they decided to convert the two parallel single lines to double track working. Crossovers were installed at Smallbrook and a signalbox was constructed from timber. When Smallbrook came in we were under Eastleigh, and Inspector Bennett who was a rare old one for speed. In fact, the box was in operation before the roof was on! The first signalmen to operate the signalbox were a chap called Green and Jimmy Hooper from Newport.

Smallbrook Junction Signalbox was only open for the summer service to operate the double line into Ryde St. John's Road, and control the junction, so during the winter service the double track reverted to two single lines operated by Ryde St. John's Signalbox. It is doubtful if any other signalbox in Great Britain operated in such a unique way.

The changeover and closing of Smallbrook for the winter was done during the quiet period of train services between Saturday night and early Sunday morning.

Some preliminary work would be undertaken at St. John's Road on the Friday, when the two signal arms for the Newport Road along with the home signal arm for the Ventnor Road were replaced. Crosses were placed over the arms to indicate to drivers that they were 'out of use'.

After the departure of the last train from Ryde St. John's Road on a Saturday night, the signals on the gantry at Ryde were brought into use. Then work on the crossover pointwork at St. John's was started. During the summer service all this pointwork was locked and the rods to St. John's Road Box removed. For the winter the reverse was done, with a member of Sid Newberry's Permanent Way gang unlocking the points, while my Signalling and Telegraph people would replace the connecting rods.

We then used to have a cup of tea and just wait for the last train to come up from Brading. As soon as the engine was in the shed, we would put a trolley on the lines and push it off to Smallbrook. Our first stop was at Smallbrook down distant signal, where the arm would be taken down, numbered and placed on the trolley. The same would be done with the home signal a little further down.

As soon as the eight or so of us in the working party arrived at Smallbrook, one gang would set off with the trolley to dismantle the outer home and distant signals. Meanwhile, another gang would dismantle the signals close to the box. This left me and a colleague to dismantle the token equipment. When the trolley arrived back, we would stack the signal arms in the corner of Smallbrook Box, numbered and labelled. Sid Newberry's P.W. men would then padlock the crossover pointwork, and we would lock the signalbox door.

The trolley then went back home to St. John's Road Box, where I had the job of reconnecting the token instruments, and changing the track diagram in the box. After a warm cup of tea, I would then make a thorough test of the Ryde – Haven Street and Ryde – Brading section equipment. It was all a piece of cake and never went wrong. We would be happily finished four hours after starting. A few days after, Mr Fidler and Jimmy James, the outside carpenter, would walk up to Smallbrook and nail the shutter up over the windows. The signalbox would then be left to the wildlife until we opened it up the following year. All that is left of the box today is the concrete base, but, who knows, perhaps the wooden structure of Smallbrook Junction Signalbox may be re-erected at Haven Street Steam Centre one day?

I treasure my memories, and look back at the whole bunch of railwaymen on the Isle of Wight as a family. It was a real joy working together.

Jimmy James

Signal fitters were a very essential part of the old Isle of Wight railways system. Their job consisted of the maintenance of signals, points and crossing gate locks. They could be called out in any weather or at any time of the day or night.

Signals especially, needed a great deal of constant care and adjustment as hot and cold weather affected the wir-

One of the most unusual signals on the Isle of Wight, pictured outside Ventnor West Station.
J. A. Britton

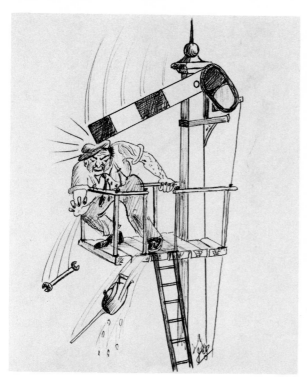

The signal fitter, by Jimmy James

ing. Sometimes they dropped slightly when they should have been at danger – this, of course, only affected the distant signals as the connecting wire reached up to half a mile in length.

Modern quadrant signals now stay level at danger and rise upwards for safety. The old type were just the opposite and, if the fitters were not careful, they could have dropped when they shouldn't.

G. A. Hunt

The following is as prepared in 1929:

Signalling in the Isle of Wight

Signalling modes, and equipment have been considerably improved in the Isle of Wight, since amalgamation of the Island Companies into the Southern Railway Group. I do not propose in this article to deal with previous modes of signalling, as it would involve a considerable amount of space, but will deal with each Signal Box, and its relative section, (excluding goods yards, and siding connections) as operated at the present time. Unless otherwise stated all stations that are controlled by a signal box, are provided with Distant, Home and Starting Signals, and all Level Crossing Gates, with the exception of two situated on the Freshwater Branch Line, are protected by fixed signals.

Ryde Pier Head 'The gateway to the Isle of Wight'. The signal box, (28 Levers 7 Spares) controls the Pier Head with its three platform roads, and Esplanade Station, the latter by means of an outer home signal (up road), and an advance starting signal (down road), both situated at the leading ends of platforms, and both are track circuited. An advance starting signal is also provided between Ryde Pier Head platform starting signals, and the advance starting signal situated at the Esplanade Station (down road). The block section is with Ryde St. Johns Road, (double line) operated with S. R. standard three position instruments.

Ryde St Johns Road. (40 Levers 7 Spare) The block sections are with Brading, (single line) and Haven Street, (single line) both sections are operated by Electric Train Staff. During the summer months the block section is with Smallbrook Junction, double line) operated with S. R. standard three position instruments. The following are track circuited, up advance starting to Ryde Pier Head, down home signals, and the diverging points to the two down platform roads. The up home signals from Brading and Haven Street, are electrically locked with crossover roads points, situated between these signals and the starting signal.

Smallbrook Junction. (20 Levers 5 Spare) Opened during summer months. By the provision of a scissor crossing points, at this junction, two single lines between the junction and Ryde St Johns are worked as double line, the distance being 1 mile, a great asset during the summer months. The junction is controlled on all sections, by outer and inner home signals. A treadle is provided at the from Ryde down outer home signal, operating an instrument in the signal box showing (Train waiting at outer home), also locking the block instrument, when signal is at danger and a train passes over treadle.

Brading. (30 Levers 1 Spare) Controls the Bembridge Branch (single line), which terminates at Brading in Bay Road, a through controlled road from branch to Sandown Main Line is also provided. The Branch is operated by the Train Staff (one engine in steam). Also block section with Sandown (double line) operated by S. R. standard three position instruments. An advance starting signal to Sandown is also provided and track circuited.

Sandown. (32 Levers) An up to Ryde advance starting signal is provided at this station. Controls the Newport Line which terminates in a Bay Road, a through controlled road is also provided from Newport Line to Shanklin Main Line. (See Merstone Junction for block working of this line). Also block section with Shanklin (single line), operated with Electric Train Staff. The signal box is situated in the centre of the up platform, projecting through the station roof. Those who are acquainted with staff changing at crossing places will, appreciate the value, and the time saved by this central position.

Shanklin. (20 Levers 5 Spare) The block section is also with Wroxall (single line) operated with Electric Train Staff. The signal box is situated on the up platform in a central position.

Wroxall. (12 Levers 1 Spare). The block section is also

with Ventnor (single line) operated with Electric Train Staff. An unique feature at this signal box, which is combined with booking office, is that the starting signals are electrically locked with the Staff Instruments, the levers operating these signals cannot be pulled off unless a staff has been withdrawn.

Ventnor. This is the terminus for the Ryde Ventnor Section, (15 Levers 2 Spare) controlling two platform roads. The two arrival signals are situated inside the tunnel, being Seimens electric light signals, worked in conjunction with the levers in signal box application to them. Any failure of these signals is denoted by a buzzer in the signal box.

To return to Ryde St Johns Road on to *Haven Street*, which is a combined signal box and booking office (16 Levers 3 Spare). The block section is also with Whippingham (single line) operated with Tyers No. 2 Tablet Instruments.

Whippingham. (11 Levers 1 Spare) combined signal box, and booking office. The block section is also with Newport South (single line) operated with Tyers No. 2 Tablet Instruments.

Newport South. (20 Levers 1 Spare) controls Newport station with Newport North (double line & up loop line). The sections are operated with Preece two position instruments, also block section with Shide (single line) operated with Tyers No. 4 Tablet Instruments. This signal box controls the opening and closing of the drawbridge over the River Medina, which carries the Newport to Ryde, and Sandown single lines. The machinery controlling the movement of the drawbridges is electrically locked by two special levers in the signal box, which are interlocked with the fixed signals. The two special levers cannot be operated unless the Shide-Newport, and Whippingham-Newport Electric Train Tablets are inserted in the Annetts locks which are fitted on these levers.

Newport North. (36 Levers) Controls the north end of Newport Station, the running lines already mentioned at the south box, and a bay road used by the Freshwater and Cowes local trains. A down to Cowes advance starting, and an up from Cowes outer home signals are also provided. The up from Cowes inner home signals, are electrically locked with the diverging points of main, and loop lines, situated between these signals and the starting signals. The block section is also with Cowes (single line) operated with Tyers No. 7 Tablet Instruments. An intermediate siding Tablet Instrument also being provided at Medina Wharf.

Cowes. (22 Levers) This is the terminus from Newport controlling three platform roads.

To return to Newport North, this signal box also controls with Ningwood (single line) Freshwater (single line) when Ningwood switched out of circuit. The block section is operated with Train Staff and Ticket when Ningwood is switched in circuit, Train Staff one engine in steam when

operating with Freshwater. This system of working is known as short and long staff section working.

Ningwood. (9 Levers) When switched in circuit, the block section is also with Freshwater, operating with Train staff and Ticket, the block telegraph with Newport North and Freshwater being Sykes Two position one wire instruments. The levers are in a signal box, in the centre of down platform, the instruments and Train Staff Ticket boxes being in the booking office.

Freshwater. (10 Levers 2 Spare) This is the terminus for this branch line controlling one platform road.

To return to Newport South on to *Shide*. (9 Levers) The block section is with Merstone Junction (single line) operated with Tyers No. 4 Tablet Instruments. This station is not a crossing place for passenger trains.

Merstone Junction. (28 Levers 2 Spare) What would normally be the up and down roads, are (up) No. 1, and (down) No. 2, roads at this station, a train from Newport or Sandown can be accepted, and started from either road, also trains from Sandown can run through either road. The Level Crossing Gates at this station are the only gates operated by a wheel in the signal box, in the Isle of Wight, all others being by hand. The main line block section is also with Newchurch when switched in circuit, with Sandown when Newchurch switched out, operated with Train Staff (Sandown and Merstone) and Ticket, the block telegraph being Preece Two position one wire instruments.

Newchurch. (8 Levers 2 Spare) Signal box, and booking office combined, is an intermediate block telegraph post, non crossing place. The down direction road is only provided with Distant, and Home signals. Two signal frames at this signal box, are utilised as one frame.

To return to Merstone Junction, ordinary scheduled trains for the Ventnor West Branch, depart and terminate from No. 2 Road at this station. The block section is also with Whitwell when switched out, operated with Train Staff and Ticket with Whitwell, Train Staff (one engine in steam) with Ventnor West. The block telegraph is Preece Two position one wire instruments.

Whitwell. (10 Levers 1 Spare) When switched in circuit, the block section is also with Ventnor West, operated with Train Staff and Ticket. The levers are in a signal box, situated at the end of down platform, the instruments and Train Staff Ticket boxes are in the booking office.

Ventnor West. (13 Levers 2 Spare) This is the terminus for this branch line, controlling two platform roads. The locking of the levers at this signal box are so arranged so as to allow the points to be set, and the home and starting signals to be lowered for one road, for the working of a push and pull train, to arrive and depart when carrying the Long Section Train Staff, with no attendance at the signal box. The locking and releasing of these two signals are operated by a special lever, and a Annetts Lock in the signal box, the Long Section Train staff being used to

Engine No. 28 *Ashey*, with Driver Harold Lacey at the controls, ready to depart with a train for Merstone Junction and Sandown in 1929. In that year the lower storey of the station building at Newport was rebuilt by the Southern Railway — when platforms 1 and 2 were extended at the northern end of the station.   *George H. Hunt*

No. 33 *Bembridge* leaves Newport with a Sandown – Cowes two coach stopping train in Janury 1956. A train for Ryde has just left Platform 3 and can be seen disappearing over the Medina Drawbridge on the left of the picture.

Dr Gerald R. Siviour

operate the Annetts Lock. The levers are in a signal box at the end of No. 1 platform the instruments and Train Staff Ticket box are in the booking office.

In concluding this article, a more interesting collection of signalling modes, coupled with their complicated connecting points, on single lines, would be hard to find elsewhere on the Southern Railway, with only approximately 3 miles of double line, and 53 miles of single line.

Jim Foster

When I left the Army I went as a standby at Medina Wharf for the Isle of Wight Central Railway. Eventually I was lucky enough to be transferred to Newport as a station cleaner; this was when Mr Young was the stationmaster. Again with my luck running for me I became a porter.

I soon made friends with another porter, Charley Aldridge. Going up the platform one day, I watched Charley pushing an old lady in a bath chair towards the track crossing at the Cowes end of the station. There was a lot of grease down the ramp as he was going across. Suddenly, he capsized her and turned her right out on to the grease. The old lady just got up and walked across by herself. She turned to Charley and said, 'That's the best cure I have had. Here is half a crown.'

It was at Newport that I had a bookmaking business for the horses which I inherited from Joe Snellgrove. I used to take bets off everyone on the railway, from P. W. men to Inspectors like Mr Ranger and Mr Booth. A fireman coming on duty at Newport Loco Depot gave me a tip that the police were waiting for me at the railway approach, as running a 'book' was quite illegal! I therefore took avoiding action and went up the yard and down the river where someone rowed me across. The betting slips were in cushion tyre of my bicycle. If the Police had stopped me they wouldn't have found a thing on me. I did well, and Jack Horner won the Grand National giving me a clear book. Eventually it got too hot for me, and like Joe Snellgrove, I had to pass the book on to someone else.

Ron A. Bennett

I can say that I was born and bred on the Isle of Wight railways. I was born in the Station House at Ningwood on the Freshwater, Yarmouth and Newport Railway. My father was stationmaster at Ningwood, and later Newport FYN Station, so Isle of Wight steam railways were in my blood. My earliest recollection of life at Ningwood Station was a visit by the Divisional Superintendent from Newport. It was night time and darkness was falling, when my father received a tip off to say the Superintendent was on his way. Unfortunately, the distant signal at the end of the station was minus its lamp. Immediately my father sent the old Permanent Way ganger, Mr Drower, down to the signal with a lamp before the official from Newport arrived. Before the ganger could get to the distant signal he saw the lights of the train, and dodged out of the way into a hedge. Meanwhile the train passed and the Divisional Superintendent observed that the distant signal light was out. Upon arriving at the station, he notified my father about the signal lamp and said it

would not do! In the meantime the old ganger had replaced the lamp, and disappeared off into the fields. My father escorted the Superintendent out on to the platform where the signal could clearly be seen. Lo and behold, there was a light! That man was full of apologies. If only he had known what had gone on!

It was natural that I should follow in my father's footsteps and work on the Island railways. Well, I started off as a porter/guard, and shall never forget my first day. I was guard on the Cement Train between Shide and the Cement Mills on the Cowes Road. We cut the engine off, a small Terrier Tank, and opened the gates to the siding. Meanwhile, I should have applied the brakes, but being a 'rookie' I was unaware of the procedure. Being a downhill gradient into the Cement Mills siding, the wagons moved off, gaining speed all the way. Fortunately, the wagons jumped off the track at the points, but as they were fully loaded with chalk the derailment sent up a white cloud over the surrounding area. At the Newport Office the Superintendent said he would overlook the incident as it was my first day; that was July, 1938.

During the early part of the Second World War there was a local Home Guard platoon based at Newport Station — a keener bunch you have never seen. One Tuesday night whilst on duty at Newport Signalbox I witnessed a very amusing incident involving the 'Dad's Army'. Members of the platoon were playing cards in the waiting room, when suddenly there was an almighty commotion. Empty milk churns started rolling around the platform and the Home Guard got their guns and dashed out ready to stop an enemy invasion. 'It's Gerry!' shouted one. However, upon closer inspection they discovered an escaped pig from the cattle pen. One had to be very careful with the Home Guard during darkness. For instance, one night I was going on duty through the Freshwater Yard to the station. I had forgotten that a Home Guard sentry was on patrol until I heard,''alt — 'oo goes 'err?' Unfortunately, the sentry must have had a few too many whiskies and I had to move very quickly flat on to my face, otherwise I would have received some lead!

During the latter part of the War in 1944, I was called upon to be a guard on the last train from Newport to Cowes. We pulled into Mill Hill Station, the last stop before entering Cowes. At Mill Hill, the platform was on a curve, and I looked out of my guard's compartment down the train. Then I walked across to check the other side of the train before departing. To my amazement, I saw a number of carriage doors open with American G I soldiers standing in a row answering the call of nature, after an evening of sampling the local brew! Opposite the station was an appreciative audience of ladies in their houses, delighted at this unexpected extravaganza!

For some time I was based out at Merstone Junction Signalbox, where I had a lot of fun. I remember on one afternoon, the branch train coming into the station from Ventnor West, and the driver of the engine came up into the box to see me. 'I've knocked a pheasant down at Godshill. It's an hour's wait until the next train. Can I go back and collect it?' the driver said. Well, I took a chance and gave him the staff, in the hope that I would not be caught by the Divisional Superintendent. He showed me the bird when he returned — it was a smasher!

On another occasion at the same station, the grade one porter Jack Smith, had played a trick on me. Now being determined to even the score, I set about paying him back one night by sabotaging the station oil lamps which were Jack's pride and joy. I waited until it was dark, and then climbed up a long ladder to get an old bird's nest from the tall trees next to the signalbox. I then collected a shovel full of cow dung from the field and dropped it into the nest. Finally, I placed the bird's nest and its contents on top of the station lamp. The next morning a waiting passenger for the 8.43a.m. train to Newport drew Jack's attention to the spectacle. Immediately the proud porter climbed a ladder to remove the nest and rectify the appearance of his station. He caught hold of the bird's nest with such a force that its contents cascaded down over him. The waiting passenger commented, 'Well, I have heard of birds feathering their own nests, but it's the first time I've seen this!'

I finished my signalling days at Newport North Box and remained there from 1951 until it closed in 1966. One afternoon while I was on duty there, a train came in from Medina Wharf. The driver and fireman had lost the token in the coal, and unfortunately threw it into the engine's fire in a shovel full of coal. When they arrived at Newport they unhooked the wagons and disappeared up the yard. The crew dropped the fire and discovered the red hot remains of the token in the cinders. They placed the metal token in a bucket of water to cool it down. Nothing was ever said about the incident — until now! So much water has passed under the bridge, so it does not matter if I relate the story, but at the time we would all have been sacked!

Jimmy James

Before Ron joined the Freight Department and eventually finished up at Ryde St. John's Road, he was a signalman at Newport in the North Box. Many Island railwaymen can picture him leaning out of the box window and hear his stentorian voice echoing all over Newport yard.

Jim Hooper

I was fifty-two years working on the Island railways, during which time I worked in every signalbox in the Island while they were open. I was also used to relieve the area inspectors when they were away on holiday or sick, and finished up as station supervisior at Ryde Pier Head for the last six years of my career.

Although I started at Wootton and was later at Haven Street, my regular signalbox was Newport North Box for some time. This was interesting to work as it had thirty six levers controlling the north end of Newport Station running lines, a bay road used by Freshwater and Cowes local trains, and the block section for the single line to Cowes (including the intermediate siding Tablet Instrument for Medina Wharf). Before they closed the various lines on the Island this was a very busy box to work in. During the early part of the Second World War, I received a phone call from Monty Taylor at Whippingham to inform me that enemy aircraft were approaching Newport. My reply from the North Box at Newport was something like this, 'Yes, Monty, I know, they're machine gunning the box!'

From Newport I went on to the relief staff, but I always enjoyed returning home for short spells. There were such lively characters on the station. For instance on one occasion Bert Pullinger, the station foreman got me to trick 'Putt' Richardson who was always scrounging tea. Instead of tea we gave him crushed dog tablets, but he still drank it in hot water. Everyone joined in the fun on the Island railways.

Ron Bennett by Jimmy James

A busy time at Newport Station as No. 20 *Shanklin* waits to leave for Ryde, while No. 14 *Fishbourne* enters with a train for Cowes. The remains of the partially demolished Newport – Sandown viaduct are pictured to the right of the signal.

R. J. Blenkinsop

Terry Wright exchanges the single line tokens with Driver Tony Tiltman at Haven Street on 4 October 1965. Driver Tiltman's engine, No. 24 *Calbourne* pictured hauling the 9.18a.m. to Cowes, is now preserved in working order at Haven Street.

John Goss

James Blenkinsop, seated on the Medina Bank, views the preserved No. 24 *Calbourne* drifting across the Medina Drawbridge at Newport. Fireman Joe Maxfield has made an effort to clean the British Railways locomotive crest on the side tank of *Calbourne* — Isle of Wight fashion:

R. J. Blenkinsop

The Assistant for the Isle of Wight and his staff at Newport Station in the Southern Railway era. Back row: Newport Stationmaster Hawkins, Stores Superintendent Doughty, Office Boy Chambers, Locomotive Foreman Bale, Chief Clerk Prismall, Clerical Officer Clark, Clerical Officer Wheeler, Traffic Inspector Churchill. Front row: Clerk Beasley, Assistant for the Isle of Wight Mr. Bell, Unknown.

Jimmy James Collection

A Cowes – Newport train hauled by No. 17 *Seaview* passes Wirral Farm on the banks of the River Medina. Note the barge on the river.

R. J. Blenkinsop

Two stations seldom mentioned on Island railway timetables were Cement Mills Halt and Medina Wharf Halt. Both were situated between Newport and Mill Hill. Pictured is Medina Wharf Halt which was a wooden platform, barely fifteen feet long with an electric light. The halt was mainly used by workmen for the Wharf. Trains only stopped at the halt if prior request was made to the guard, and it was necessary to occupy the compartment next to the loco-motive. To make the return trip, it was possible to stop the train by flagging down the driver,

Timothy P. Cooper

No. 18 *Ningwood* after leaving Medina Wharf Junction with a coal train for Newport in 1964.

Timothy P. Cooper

Drummond boilered '02' No. 31 *Chale* drifts into Mill Hill with a four coach train to Cowes in August 1965. The train has just passed over Smithard's Lane Crossing — just out of view around the curve.

Timothy P. Cooper

Mill Hill Station in 1932. The station platform was located on a sharp curve and served the residential suburbs of Cowes.

George H. Hunt

Mill Hill Station by Jimmy James.

No. 20 *Shanklin* bursts out of the gloomy 208 yard long Mill Hill tunnel at the southern end of the station. *Shanklin* was hauling an up empty carriage stock train straight through Mill Hill — non-stop to Newport in January 1966. Meanwhile, on the platform, Porter Horace Cade appears to be undisturbed and continues with his cleaning duties.

Timothy P. Cooper

Christmas 1964, but where are the trains? The Isle of Wight's two leading train spotters in steam days; left, Timothy P. Cooper and, right, Mike 'Chuff' Downer. We have so much to thank these two remarkable gentlemen for — Tim for his photographic and historical documentation of the Island railways and 'Chuff' for his unstinting efforts with the preservation of the Island's steam heritage at Haven Street. Thank you, gentlemen!

Timothy P. Cooper Collection

No. 26 *Whitwell* coasts down the 1:67 gradient from Mill Hill tunnel into Cowes.

Dr Gerald R. Siviour

No. 20 *Shanklin* passing over Binney Bridge, Cowes, with a train for Ryde Pier Head in the summer of 1965. The photograph portrays something of the character of the Isle of Wight Railway in a typical Island town setting.

Timothy P. Cooper

Cowes Station in 1929, some fourteen miles from Ryde Pier Head. This was the terminus of the Island's first railway, the Cowes and Newport Railway, which opened on 16 June 1862.

George H. Hunt

No. 20 *Shanklin* rounds the curve into Cowes Station with a train from Ryde Pier Head.

R. J. Blenkinsop

The surviving '02' tank No. 24 *Calbourne*, which is now happily preserved, trundles into Cowes Station with a train from Sandown in January 1956. Passenger trains always used Platform 1, Platform 2 being pressed into use for Cowes Firework Night Excursions and for similar extra trains.

Dr Gerald R. Siviour

No. 20 *Shanklin* backs the empty coaches up the gradient at Cowes Station prior to running round.

R. J. Blenkinsop

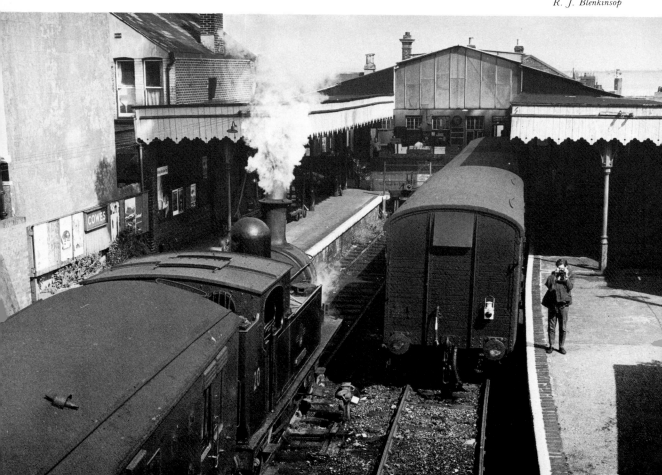

Cowes Station concourse.

R. J. Blenkinsop

The glass-roof concourse at Cowes Station was spacious and the floral displays brought much favourable comment from passengers. Of the various station departments pictured, the refreshment room was closed and the W. H. Smith bookstall opened only in the summer.

Jimmy James

The exterior of Cowes station. The station was almost unaltered from its original condition when it closed in 1966. It stood at the junction of Terminus Road and Corvel Lane on a sloping site.

Timothy P. Cooper

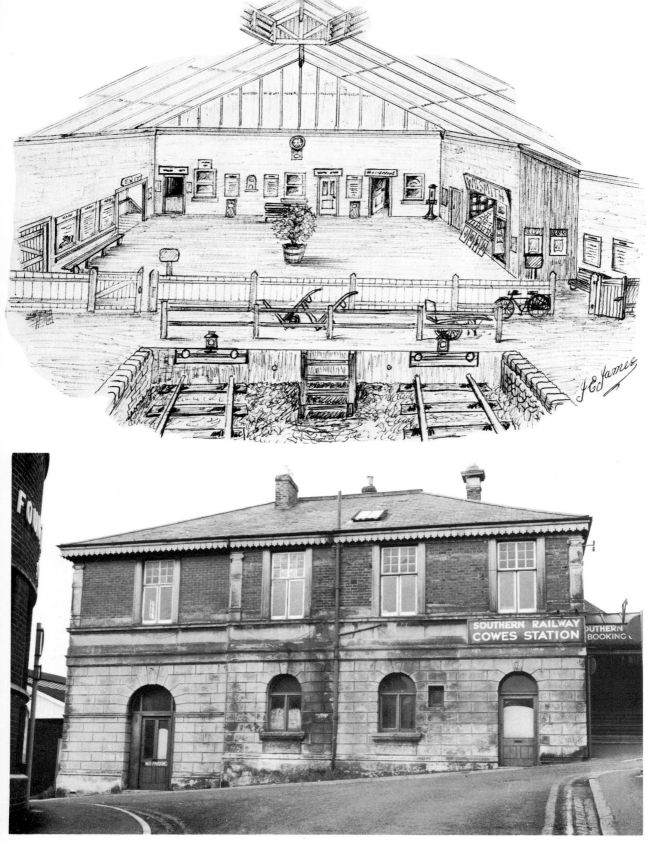

The stairs up to the booking office were a typical Southern wooden structure The small faded notice on the righthand pillar stated that there was an entrance on the level a little further on.

Timothy P. Cooper

Chapter Six ~ The Freshwater Branch
(Newport-Yarmouth-Freshwater)

SOUTHERN RAILWAY

INSTRUCTION No. 11a, (1926).

S 8945

SPECIAL INSTRUCTIONS AS TO THE METHOD OF DEALING WITH TRAIN STAFFS AND TICKETS ON THE FRESHWATER BRANCH IN CONNECTION WITH THE WORKING OF THE MORNING MAIL TRAIN.

1. On Weekdays, Monday to Friday inclusive, and Sundays, the Driver of the last up train at night from Freshwater is authorised to take the Freshwater—Ningwood train staff through to Newport. Upon arrival at Newport he must surrender it to the Station Master, or person in charge of the staff working at that place, together with the Ningwood—Newport train staff.

2. After the last up train, Saturdays excepted, has cleared Freshwater, the Station Master, or person in charge, at that place must see that the road is set and the down home signal lowered before leaving duty.

3. After the last up train, Saturdays excepted, has cleared Ningwood, the Station Master, or person in charge, at that place must see that the road is set and all down signals lowered before leaving duty.

4. Before leaving Newport the Driver of the morning mail train must be handed by the Station Master, or person in charge of the staff working, the Newport—Ningwood and Ningwood—Freshwater train staffs, and be instructed that block signalling is not in operation and to proceed with caution.

5. The mail train must stop short of the crossing gates at Calbourne and the Guard will open them and lower the necessary signal for the train to proceed. The Driver will then draw his train past, and stop well clear of, the gates, after which the Guard will replace the down home signal to danger and close the gates across the railway and the Driver will retain the Newport—Ningwood train staff, which he will take through to Freshwater.

6. The Crossing Keepers at Petticoat Lane, Pound, Hill Place and Freshwater Causeway will be held responsible for seeing that the crossing gates are open for the passage of the train.

7. The Driver of the first up train in the morning from Freshwater will carry both the Freshwater—Ningwood and Ningwood—Newport train staffs, unless the conditions laid down in paragraph 9 of this instruction apply, and strict block signalling must be observed.

8. Upon arrival of the first up train from Freshwater at Ningwood, the Station Master, or person in charge, of the staff working at that place, will collect from the Driver the Freshwater—Ningwood train staff in the usual way together with the Newport—Ningwood ticket if the conditions in paragraph 9 have applied, and he will be held responsible for satisfying himself by personal observation that the Driver holds the Ningwood—Newport train staff, before the train is allowed to leave Ningwood.

9. Should it be necessary for a train to follow the Mail train from Newport to Ningwood after the Signal Boxes have been opened, the Driver of the Mail train will be given the Ningwood—Freshwater staff as detailed above but will only be shown the Newport—Ningwood Staff and will proceed to Ningwood with a Ticket which he must retain until he reaches Ningwood on the return trip from Freshwater, when the ticket must be handed to the Station Master, or person in charge, in exchange for the staff of the Ningwood—Newport section.

WATERLOO STATION,

23rd July, 1926.

EDWIN C. COX,

Chief Operating Superintendent.

(R. 1.693).

Special instructions for the Freshwater Branch.

Mrs Kit Attrill

My mother, Mrs M. E. Prouten was stationmistress at Watchingwell Station for about twenty years, at the wage of 7s 6d per week. My father who died at an early age worked on the permanent way and my two brothers, when old enough, became drivers.

Watchingwell was known as a halt and trains only stopped if requested. You had to tell the driver or the guard if you wanted to stop there. My mother had to work a hand signal if anyone wanted to get on the train. One of my brothers had to climb up the signal once a week to bring the lamps down. They were then sent to Newport Office to be cleaned and refilled with long burning oil before being returned. The two lamps on the platform were cleaned and refilled every day by my mother. The platform edge was kept white-washed, again mostly by my mother to make it look clean and smart.

Watchingwell was on the Simion Estate, and it was not unusual for Lady Laura Simion to pay us visit. Her friends and relations used the train frequently when visiting Swainstone House.

On leaving Watchingwell the next stop was Calbourne and between the two the track ran through woodland. During the early 1920s pheasants were bred on the estate for winter sport, and on several occasions the train would hit one and injure it — the driver would stop the next time through and tell my mother. If we were lucky enough to find it, we had pheasant for dinner.

The last train from Newport to Freshwater was the 8.30 p.m. and there was one guard by the name of Mr G. Brown who would have the train stop at Watchingwell and give my brothers a return ride in the guard's van for company which, I might add, was a great treat.

Early one dark winter evening some horses broke down the fence of their field and wandered on to the track. Being dark, the next train injured one or two of them and my mother had to walk about half a mile along the track and place detonators on the rail to warn of danger.

The railway allowed my mother one ton of coal a year to burn in the office. The office was in fact also our kitchen where the tickets were sold through a trap that opened into the waiting room. It cost my mother 3 pence a week, on Saturdays, to travel to Newport on a private ticket to do her weekly shopping.

Maurice Prouten

With my sister Kit, and my brother, we used the train to travel to school at Carisbrooke and did so until the end of our school days. I remember that as there was no piped water laid on to the station house at Watchingwell, mother often obtained a bath of hot water from the locomotives for her washing. The two regular engines of the Freshwater, Yarmouth and Newport Railway were No. 1 *Medina* and No. 2 *Freshwater*, but there was also a small 20hp Drewry petrol railcar. This odd vehicle was driven by Bert Falick who was also the guard.

At Watchingwell we had two standard lamps on the platform which had to be lit every evening. In rough weather at times this task was difficult, and there were also the signal lamps to be lit every evening which caused a few swear words at times.

Very early one morning we were awakened by the mail train that stopped at the station, and a lot of noise was going on. It appears that they had run out of water and were getting water with buckets from our pond for the engine. They arrived back later with the school train, so it appears they won their way to Freshwater.

On another occasion in that period, a train had arrived at Newport with a door open and a lady's belongings were on the seat. Not knowing what exactly had happened they ordered a fullscale search to be made. I went out with my father and not very far from our home at Watchingwell Station we discovered a young lady lying on the bank. I don't think she was injured at all, and she spent the night at Watchingwell with us.

Mrs Katie Buckett

Although I was not employed by the railway, my parents Mr and Mrs W. H. Henley between them were in charge of Calbourne and Shalfleet village railway station for forty one years.

My father commenced his railway career as parcels office boy at Ryde St. John's Road Station in 1885 when he was 12 years of age. His father was an engine driver, and I have heard my aunt say that long before he started work he would be missing, but they knew where to find him - he would be sitting on the loo studying his father's Rule Book. He remembered that one of the first instructions given him as parcels office boy was that a news letter usually sent to the *County Press* newspaper on Fridays by their Ryde correspondent, Mr W. H. Dann J. P. (who later became Editor of the paper), must on no account be forgotten.

Dad later worked at most of the stations on the Isle of Wight Railway, and then as audit clerk at Ryde St. John's Road until he transferred to the Isle of Wight Central Railway in 1902. He was appointed stationmaster at Calbourne and continued in that post until deafness necessitated his retirement in 1925. He was succeeded as station attendant by my mother, but he continued with clerical work for the Southern Railway doing monthly accounts, etc.

At the time the Southern Railway decided to dispense with all the stationmasters at intermediate stations; they were given promotion to mainland stations. It was very sad for my father to see his friends go. The Southern gave my father a pension of £1 a week and paid my mother 35s a week. When my father reached state pension age the Southern Railway deducted 10s from his pension. My mother had no option therefore but to take the position at Calbourne to keep a home going. The rent was low for the small bungalow containing two bedrooms, a living room with a cooking range, coal fired, a scullery with sink and copper, but we did have water laid on by tap and water cisterns in the loos. There were only two houses with that luxury in the village, the Manor House and the Vicarage, so we were lucky.

I have two younger sisters, the youngest of whom was three when my mother took over the duties, so she was

A cartoon of an actual happening on the Freshwater Line. Sufficient proof that all Island lines should have been doubled?

This portrays a gentleman of the Permanent Way Department, preparing a lineside banquet. Like footplatemen, Permanent Way staff often had a 'fry-up' on the shovel.

Some found railway terminology rather difficult to understand. The left handed ganger may be identifiable to Island railway staff.

127

"WHATS THEM FOR?"

"WELL, YOU DID SAY BRING ALONG A COUPLE OF CHAIRS GANGER"

— THE NEW RECRUIT —

This illustrates that some new recruits for the Permanent Way Department were perhaps a little naïve. Shades of 'rubber hammers and sky hooks!'

tied up with responsibilities until she retired in 1944.

My father had been stationmaster at several Island stations before taking over Calbourne. He had been posted to Wroxall for some time, when one evening he discovered he was getting short of coal for the office fire, and he took a broom out when the coal train passed through and tried to knock a lump off with no success. However, the broom lodged on a truck and it had a free ride via Sandown and Merstone to Newport. He had to keep quiet about it, but years after he was speaking of the incident when an ex-railway man said 'That's where that broom came from.' Apparently he was at Newport Station when the truck came in with the broom hanging on. It was a great mystery for some time where a domestic type broom could have come from.

Where there were crossing gates the stationmasters had to stay on duty until the last train had gone through. Sometimes ballast trains would rattle through Calbourne until 2a.m. in the morning.

My father's hobby was playing the violin, when his hearing was good, and the other stationmasters along the Freshwater Line would take off their telephone receivers while he played to them.

When my father was in hospital we had all the oil lamps to clean and refill. It was not long burning oil in the Freshwater, Yarmouth and Newport days, so this was an every-other-day job. We had four signal lamps, two distant signals, two lamps on the platform, one in the waiting room and two on the four gates spanning the public highway - so it was quite a long job to do in the oil shed with wicks to trim, etc. One evening I said I would do the ladder work (I hated heights), as my mother was suffering from a migraine that day. I took the lamp in one

hand, and held on like grim death to the side of the iron ladder with the other hand. Being nervous of the height I was holding the lamp at all angles, but in so doing I annointed my mother's head with oil before she had time to move. I also had to operate the crossing gates which were heavy to push in rough weather. They bolted in the road and were locked by a lever in the signalbox.

On Saturdays two trains were run to Newport at a cheap fare for marketing (6d return). These trains were crowded and some of the male passengers were 'pretty' by the time they came back on the last train. Often my mother had to assist the butler from Westover House (who was a regular on Saturday nights) into our living room, away from aggressive passengers from another village and keep him there until the all clear. Incidentally the people living at Westover House in the village were the Moulton-Barretts, descendants of the Elizabeth Barrett Browning family. Her brother is buried in Calbourne churchyard.

Newport ran a cattle market in the centre of town. Tuesday was market day and cattle trucks were shunted on to the back of the first train in the morning which was the school train, too. Sometimes it was like a cowboy film: animals seldom go where you want them to, so often they dodged down the platform on to the track, with farmers, guard and my father chasing them. Quite often one would escape into a field and my sisters and I were very late for school along with the other pupils, but we had a good excuse.

My mother was frequently called upon to provide first aid. A young lady opened her umbrella after alighting from the train, and walked across in front of the engine. It was a stormy night and the driver saw her put up the umbrella and thought how silly on a night like that. She was crossing to a small swing gate which led to the road, when the wind took the umbrella, took her up the track and she was knocked by the buffer on to the railway bank. The driver was unaware of the accident until they discovered parts of the umbrella on the engine on arrival at Newport. She was heard crying out and brought into my mother's room. The doctor from Newport was sent for and he inserted sixteen stitches in her head and she had back injuries and was in hospital for a long time.

On another occasion I had been shopping, and returning on the midday train, as it approached Calbourne about a mile away, it came to a halt. Windows in the carriage dropped and heads popped out. There was the driver, 'Smiler' Ted Dale leaning out of the engine with a piece of steam coal in his hand taking aim at a beautiful cock pheasant running along the railway bank, but he missed, and I was glad! If Driver Dale was on the mail train on Good Fridays he would tie a penny and a hot cross bun on a piece of string and leave it swinging on the front door handle. He often jumped off the engine, and tapped our window and pointed down the line saying, 'Nice lot of mushrooms in the second field down.' I used to take a basket and gather them to give to him on his next trip. There was always plenty of mushrooms around the field near the station.

A day or two after the 1914-18 War was declared an army officer and six men alighted from the last train. They had been sent for duty at a viaduct between Calbourne and the next station, Ningwood. The soldiers had no idea where they were coming to and had no food and no cooking utensils. Mother had to come to their rescue and our larder was bare that night. I went to the farm nearby and was able to get milk, butter and eggs. My mother boiled the eggs hard for them and gave them food and drink. The viaduct was an isolated structure with no hut or shelter and they were posted away after a few days. When the soldiers arrived and they informed my mother that they were going, I expected to see the Germans coming down the line. I was so scared, as I was only nine years old then. Later, just before the train departed, the officer explained to my mother there had been a mistake, it had not been a viaduct they had been assigned to guard, but he thanked us for the food and help.

One thing I do vividly remember of the days of steam on the Island railways was the lamp men at Newport. They would run along the roofs of the carriages and drop in the the oil lamps, jumping from coach to coach. Often the glass bowls inside would work loose and a few times drop into the carriage and start a fire on the seats. If we travelled back home to Calbourne after dark, the corner seats seemed the safest.

I can look back to those days with warmth on life at a wayside Island station in the days of steam. We had so much with wild flowers, mushrooms, blackberries and so on, even if the firemen of the engines stoked up in the station and the black soot landed on our snowy white sheets and clothes. We would like to see them now! My sisters and I were truly 'railway children'.

Calbourne Station by Jimmy James.

No. 30 *Shorwell* with driver Monty Harvie at the controls enters Ningwood Station with a train for Newport on Sunday 18 May 1952.

Eric D. Brunton

A good view of Ningwood Station in 1932, showing the crossing loop which was brought into use so that an improved summer service could be run on the Newport – Freshwater Line.

George H. Hunt

Yarmouth Station in 1932, with an '02'-hauled Newport – Freshwater train. The passenger's clothing and station advertisements are full of character and interest — so typical of the period. Yarmouth Station (10 miles from Newport), was situated at the back of the town, but the FYNR, and later the Southern Railway, obtained some passenger traffic by offering a connection with the Lymington paddle steamer service from Yarmouth Pier.

George H. Hunt

Yarmouth Station 1930 by Jimmy James.

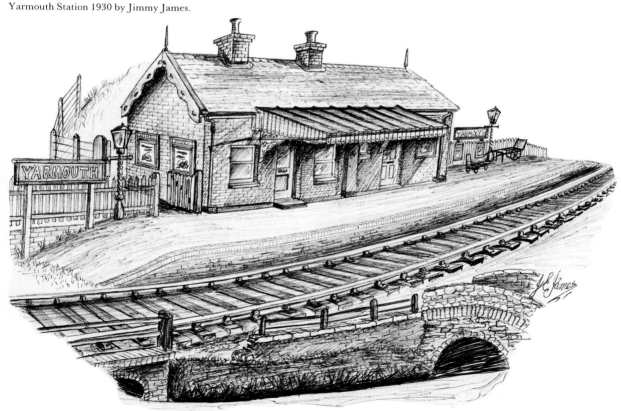

The exterior of Freshwater Station in 1927. When the line was opened, it was worked by the Isle Of Wight Central Railway Company, as the FYN posessed no engines or rolling stock! In 1913, the two companies quarrelled and the FYN hastily purchased two 0 – 6 – 0 tank engines, half a dozen carriages and a Drewry petrol railcar.

George H. Hunt

Freshwater Station by Jimmy James.

SOUTHERN RAILWAY. Stock.
787 G
$(\frac{2}{25})$
TO
WROXALL
Via PORTSMOUTH.

Gt. Western Ry.   Gt. Western Ry.
Leamington   Leamington
                    Parly.(3rd.Cls.)
TO
RYDE I. OF W.
Via Basingstoke & Stoke's Bay
11/9½ PARLY.(3rd.Cls) 11/9½
RYDE I. of W.   RYDE I. of W.
See back   T.G.

2nd · SINGLE   SINGLE · 2nd
(D.O.)   (D.O.)
Southampton Central to
Southampton Central
Ryde Esplanade   Ryde Esplanade
RYDE ESPLANADE
via Netley and Portsmouth Harbour
(S)   (S)
Fare 11/10   Fare 11/10
For conditions see over For conditions see over

Southern Railway. Stock.
787 G
$(\frac{3}{24})$
TO
VENTNOR
Via Portsmouth.

BRITISH RAILWAYS (S)
This ticket is issued subject to the Bye-laws,
Regulations and Conditions contained in the
Publications and Notices of and applicable to the
Railway Executive.
Bembridge to
WATERLOO, LONDON BRIDGE
or VICTORIA
Via Brading, Ryde & Portsmouth Harbour
THIRD CLASS   THIRD CLASS
Fare 14/1 H   Fare 14/1 H
NOT TRANSFERABLE

SOUTHERN RAILWAY. Stock.
787 G
$(\frac{2}{25})$
TO
ST. HELENS
Via PORTSMOUTH.

Gt. Western Ry.   Gt. Western Ry.
Leamington   Leamington
(R.P.)   (F.)
TO
RYDE, I. OF W.
Via Basingstoke & Stoke's Bay
25/11 FIRST CLASS 25/11
Ryde I. of W.   Ryde I. of W
SEE BACK

Great Western Railway
LEAMINGTON TO
RYDE I.W.
Via Didcot Basingstoke & Stoke's Bay
FIRST CLASS
Issued subject to the conditions & regula-
tions stated on the back hereof. (W)
Ryde I.W.   Ryde I.W.

CHEAP DAY-3rd
Ryde Pier Head
TO
SOUTHAMPTON C
or TER MINUS (for D)
Via Portsmouth Harbour
and Netley
Conditions see over

Southern Railway. Stock.
787 G
$(\frac{3}{24})$
TO
SHANKLIN
Via Portsmouth.

Postscript

The end of one era, but happily it wasn't long before the Isle of Wight Steam Railway began a new era.

A hazy morning at Haven Street. Terry Wright has just seen off No. 14 *Fishbourne* on her way to Cowes in February 1966.

Appendix One ~ War Damage on the Isle of Wight Railways

(From the Southern Railway War Damage & Incidents declassified information Files)

Air Raid Book Number One (from 3 September 1939 to 13 September 1940) is missing/presumed destroyed.

12 August 1940
VENTNOR
One bomb landed near the line between Shanklin and Wroxall and caused minor damage which was soon repaired. Two bombs were within 20 or 30 yards of the railway property and failed to explode. Due to pressure of other work the Bomb Disposal Authorities were unable to deal with the disposal of these unexploded bombs for about ten days. The matter was further complicated by the fact that the crater containing one of them fell in. The train service from Shanklin to Ventnor was suspended.

16 August 1940
At approximately 1p.m. six bombs fell on the cliffs near Ventnor Station but did not explode. The station was closed whilst the matter received the attention of the Bomb Disposal Officer. The bombs were detonated during the evening, but no damage was caused to railway property.

17 August 1940
The line between Shanklin and Ventnor was still closed due to an unexploded bomb near the line between Shanklin and Wroxall. Despite efforts to detonate it, this bomb failed to explode, and it was decided to reopen the line for normal traffic on Friday 23 August.

28 September 1940
WROXALL
A bomb fell in the vicinity of the station soon after 10p.m. The 9.45 Ryde – Ventnor was terminated at Shanklin and passengers for Wroxall and Ventnor were taken forward by taxi. The line was searched and a small quantity of debris was found on the line, but the track was not damaged. The 7.35a.m. Ryde – Ventnor will be warned to run with caution.

28 October 1940
BETWEEN NEWCHURCH AND ALVERSTONE
The track was damaged during the night (27/28 October) by a High Explosive bomb and covered with debris. There is also a suspected Delayed Action bomb about 15 yards from the track ¾ mile on the Sandown side of Newchurch. The line is out of use with a bus service between Merstone and Sandown.

28 October 1940
Push-pull working between Merstone and Newchurch. Line reopened at 3p.m.

14 November 1940
VENTNOR WEST
Delayed Action bomb fell on a bank off the Company's property about 400 yards from the station at 11.45p.m. It is 90 feet from the Whitwell road, but the report does not state what distance it is from the railway. This is being ascertained. The line is closed and a bus service in operation between St. Lawrence and Ventnor West Station. Ventnor West Station is also closed.

16 November 1940
The Military say that it is now safe to run traffic, and trains will resume with the 5.08p.m. Newport – Ventnor West.

18 November 1940
WHIPPINGHAM
A Delayed Action bomb was reported at 2a.m. 20 yards on the Newport side of the up home signal (approximately 120 yards from the station) 7 yards from the track. There are also about 15 small unexploded bombs just clear of the company's property. A bus service has been instituted between Newport and Haven Street.

18 November 1940
BETWEEN COWES AND NEWPORT
A Delayed Action bomb was discovered at 5a.m., 200 yards on the Cowes side of Cement Mills Siding. A bus service has been put into operation between Cowes and Newport. The Military advise that the Delayed Action bomb exploded on contact, and the line was re-opened at 1.08p.m.

18 November 1940
BETWEEN WHITWELL AND VENTNOR WEST
A Delayed Action bomb had been reported near the railway in the neighbourhood of St. Lawrence Tunnel. The line has been closed pending investigation. The bomb exploded during the night (17/18 November). The line remained closed from 7.11a.m. until 12.30p.m.; re-opened with 1.08p.m. Newport – Ventnor West.

Joint Report Submitted by Signalman Monty Taylor and Ray Draper
18 November 1940
WHIPPINGHAM
A total of 28 bombs were dropped in the early hours at 2a.m. as enemy planes returned from a heavy bombing raid on the Midlands. The Bomb Disposal Unit who came from Bristol, formed the opinion that a plane was damaged by Anti-Aircraft fire from the Whippingham Battery, as it was crossing the Isle of Wight. In order to gain height, the German bomber released its load. All the bombs failed to explode. A 1,000lb. Delayed

The 1000lb Delayed Action Bomb at Whippingham. 18 November 1940 at Whippingham.

Action bomb landed about 120 yards from the station, 20 yards on the Newport side of the up home signal. Twenty smaller 100lb. were found nearby in the field. We immediately closed the line and instituted a bus service between Newport and Haven Street. A further two 100 lb. bombs were found on the line and these were detonated at 5.45p.m. on 20 November. This caused four lengths of line to be destroyed and a series of telegraph poles to just blow away like match-sticks! In addition to this the cattle creep was found to be cracked. A plate-layer's trolley was used to take the 1,000lb. Delayed Action bomb away from its crater to the crossing. From here it was conveyed to King's Quay, near East Cowes for detonation. Rail traffic was resumed at 3.20p.m. on 21 November with a 5mph speed restriction.

20 November 1940
WHIPPINGHAM
A bomb exploded at 5.45p.m. So far as can be ascertained at present, four lengths of rail have been blown out, telegraph pole down and the cattle creep has been cracked. Four smaller bombs near the line are still to be exploded.

21 November 1940
WHIPPINGHAM
Traffic will not be resumed until some time tomorrow when it is anticipated repairs will be completed. the Delayed Action bombs have been declared safe by Bomb Disposal Officer. The line was restored at 3.20p.m. with a 5mph restriction.

23 November 1940
BETWEEN NEWPORT AND COWES
Police report a Delayed Action bomb near Cement Mills and state it is unsafe for traffic to pass. Line closed at 10p.m. No trace of delayed Action bomb. Line re-opened with the first train 24 November.

25 November 1940
RYDE ST. JOHN'S ROAD
A Delayed Action bomb has been reported by the police on railway property 35 yards from the track behind the coal company's store. It is in the brook below track level and screened from the line by a cement wall and coal stack. There is no effect on traffic. The Bomb Disposal Officer was unable to get at the bomb by virtue of its

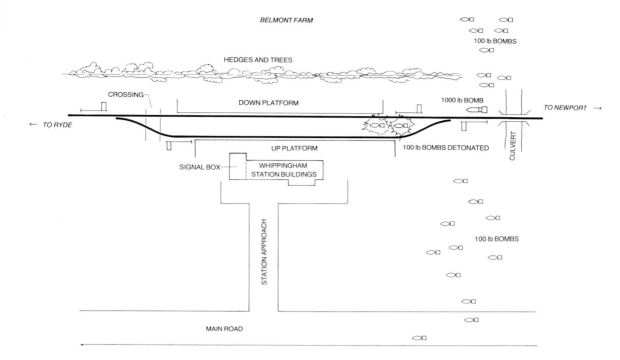

position. The bomb was declared 'safe' and left.

25 November 1940
VENTNOR WEST
The Bomb Disposal Officer has notified that it is now safe to run passenger trains. The bomb is in soft ground 400 yards from the station off the company's property.

1 December 1940
RYDE – PORTSMOUTH BOAT SERVICE
The 7.25 Portsmouth Harbour – Ryde boat will be late as the vessel was commandeered during the night to carry fire fighting appliances to Southampton. (Very heavy blitz on Southampton).

5 December 1940
BETWEEN RYDE ESPLANADE AND RYDE ST. JOHN'S ROAD
At 6.45p.m. a bomb fell on the track 4 yards north of Ryde St. John's Road damaging both lines. As a result the engine of the 6.35p.m. train Ryde Pier Head – Ventnor was derailed. No casualties. Rerailment to be effected in daylight. The engine was re-railed at 2.55 p.m. on 6 December, but the line is still blocked by damage. Line re-opened (up main and down loop) at 9a.m. on 6 December, but the down main was blocked until the afternoon.

10 January 1941
WHIPPINGHAM
A suspected Delayed action bomb fell at 12.15a.m. ½ mile Newport side of Whippingham, 45 yards from the track. A hole of two feet in diameter was produced. All railway traffic was stopped. Passenger trains termi-

nated at Wootton; and a bus service put into operation between Wootton and Newport. During the afternoon the Military stated that the bomb was a 10000lb. bomb Catergory 'B', to be left for 80 hours. Flags advised.

11 January 1941
PORTSMOUTH (Boats)
Portsmouth received a very heavy blitz during the night (10/11 January). Clarence Pier was on fire; Portsmouth Harbour unable to be used owing to a direct hit. It is impossible to ascertain whether the South Parade Pier is usable or not as the approaches may be mined. No trains are serving Portsmouth and a suggestion has been made that the boat service might operate to South-ampton. At 8.05a.m. Ryde Pier Head was instructed to hold all boats. The boat service was restored to Ports-mouth Harbour Jetty at lunch time. The Harbour Sta-tion was closed and landing stages were not usable. All steamers were undamaged, but the limited service oper-ated could only run during the hours of daylight and it was deemed desirable to route as much traffic as possible via Southampton.

16 January 1941
WHIPPINGHAM
A bomb exploded this afternoon. There was no damage to the track and line reopened at 4p.m.

11 March 1941
RYDE ST. JOHN'S ROAD
An unexploded bomb or shell was found on the down line near the north crossover at 1 mile 10 chains. All traffic suspended between Ryde Pier Head and Ryde St. John's Road. Later it was confirmed by the Military that it

was an unexploded shell about five feet deep. Emergency bus service between St. John's Road and the Esplanade where the tramway service between Esplanade and Pier Head was provided whilst removal of the shell was in progress. The line re-opened at 10.30a.m. on 12 March.

12 April 1941
SANDOWN
At about 10.15p.m. on 11 April an unexploded Anti-Aircraft shell was discovered in Newport loop at Sandown. It was reported at 1a.m. on 12 April that the ARP had removal in hand, and the area was screened with a couple of empty wagons. Push-pull services into the loop (run-round) not available), therefore a push-pull was put into use between Merstone and Sandown. The shell was subsequently found to be nose cap of a shell only and the area was declared safe at 9.30a.m.

24 May 1941
BETWEEN NEWPORT AND COWES
A series of bombs dropped at 7.20p.m. between Cement Mills Viaduct and Cement Mills Halt. The line was damaged at 11 miles 20 chains. the 7.12p.m. Newport – Cowes (engine and 3 coaches) was derailed, with no casualties. A bus service was put into operation. (Later amended to engine and 2 coaches derailed). Clearance was deferred due to suspected Delayed Action bombs in the bank. A total of 11 bombs fell in the vicinity. The Delayed Action bombs were a false alarm. Rerailing commenced at about 9.50a.m. on 25 May. The engine was rerailed at 11.30a.m. There was no crater and the track had in fact spread under the train. It is hoped to complete all repairs and re-open the line early on 26 May. Rerailing completed at 8.45p.m. The line was in order at 9.25p.m. and the train service resumed with the first train viz. 5.30a.m. goods Newport – Medina Wharf on 26 May.

28 May 1941
BETWEEN NEWPORT AND COWES
An unexploded bomb was discovered at 11.30a.m. on 27 May at 13 miles 35 chains off the Company's property. All traffic was stopped until 1.40p.m. when the Bomb Disposal Officer gave permission to pass the bomb.

20 September 1941
LOSS OF P.S. PORTSDOWN
Some time after the 4a.m. mail boat left Portsmouth Harbour a loud explosion was heard. A searchlight was played on the water and the boat was seen to be in difficulties. At 4.50a.m. the Duty Officer at the Square Tower reported that at 4.10a.m. there was a loud explosion on the water. A seachlight was played on the water, and the Portsdown was found to be in difficulties off Spitsand Fort. The service was suspended until permission to resume was given by the Admiralty at 9.10 a.m. Portsdown was split in two by the explosion in shallow water. The forward position was blown off and lying upside down. The remaining three quarters was in sufficiently shallow water that it was partially afloat. Im-

mediately after the explosion a naval pinnace went out and rescued 17 people, mostly servicemen. There were about 40 passengers aboard at the time of whom about 30 were service personel. Position at 4p.m. was as follows:

RESCUED:
Crew 3 (2 in hospital)
Service personnel 17 (4 in hospital)
Civilians 4 (actual number in hospital not known)
Total 24

BODIES RECOVERED:
Service personnel 2
Civilians 1
Total 3

MISSING:
Crew 8
Service personnel 11
Civilians number not known

The incident occurred at dead low water.

5 May 1942
COWES AREA AND MEDINA WHARF
Bombing raids on Cowes occurred from 10.45p.m. on 4 May until 12. 11a.m. on 5 May. A fire was caused at Medina Wharf causing damage to the transporters there and also some wagons. A number of bombs were also dropped near the main line, and the section from Newport was closed for examination. A number of high explosive and incendiary bombs were dropped at Medina Wharf when a lighting test was being carried out. The main switch cable for both transporters being out of use for some four weeks. At the end of that time, one transporter would be re-usable, but the other was more seriously damaged, and it was anticipated repairs would take about 10 weeks. The line between Newport and Cowes was reopened at 6.50a.m., but closed again at 12.05p.m. when an unexploded bomb was discovered 5 yards from the track at 13 miles 36 chains. The crater was 4 feet 6 inches wide by 10 feet deep. It was not possible to arrange an emergency bus service between Newport and Cowes as the roads were closed due to the presence of Delayed Action bombs.

5 May 1942
SHIDE
An unexploded bomb was discovered in the goods yard, and another about ¼ mile nearer Newport. As a result the line has been closed and a bus service put into operation between Newport and Merstone.

5/6 May 1942
COWES AREA
A bus service was arranged between Cowes and Newport commencing at 8.55p.m. on 5 May. The unexploded bomb near Medina Wharf at 13 miles 36 chains was removed south of Mill Hill at 11a.m. on 5 May. Mill Hill Station could not be used, and the service between Newport and Cowes remained suspended. The Mill Hill

bomb was found to be 'safe' and the train service was restored with the 1.08p.m. ex Newport. The phone was restored at 4.20p.m. on 6 May. The tablet took longer to restore and trains were worked with a pilotman.

13 May 1942
SHIDE
The bomb in the goods yard which fell on 5 May proved impossible to recover. The line remained totally closed until 14 May, when the line was re-opened to goods traffic, the first train being the 1.15p.m. goods Newport – Shide.

28 May 1942
SHIDE
The unexploded bomb was finally removed at 8.45p.m. on 27 May and normal working resumed with the first service on 28 May.

26 May 1942
NEWPORT
An Anti-Aircraft shell exploded in the lower goods yard causing minor damage to track and a brake third carriage in the cattle dock nearby.

10 August 1942
LYMINGTON – YARMOUTH
The *Lymington* was shelled on the 6.05p.m. passage service from Yarmouth to Lymington by an enemy aircraft. Only very minor damage was caused. Gunfire was returned by Deckhand Sticklee who was complimented by Army Officers on board. No casualties.

3 January 1943
SHANKLIN
4 bombs were dropped near the station. No damage was done to the track, but the buildings were knocked about: roof tiles displaced, windows and doors dislodged and virtually all glass broken and some ceilings down. No casualties.

17 January 1943
VENTNOR WEST
Slight damage to the signal box and station building occurred during air activity.

17 February 1943
SHANKLIN
A high explosive bomb in the vicinity caused some damage to Shanklin Station.

7 April 1943
NEWPORT
Superficial damage to the station occurred during an air raid.

26 March 1944
RYDE PIER
During landing exercises a pontoon was swept against the promenade pier and caused minor damage. The pier was closed to road traffic, but not pedestrians for part of the day.

26 April 1944
RYDE ESPLANADE AND PIER
BEMBRIDGE
ST. HELEN'S
WHITWELL
VENTNOR WEST
All received 'minor incidents'.

16 May 1944
NEWCHURCH
A High Explosive bomb dropped in the centre of the track 150 yards on the Sandown side of Newchurch Station. The crater measured 30 feet wide by 30 feet deep. About 200 feet of track was damaged. Water from the river is now flowing into the crater. Other bombs also fell near the line. A special bus service has been arranged from Merstone – Sandown. The bomb fell at about 1.30a.m. Superficial damage only to Newchurch Station. Difficulties have been experienced with water in the crater. The roof of Newchurch Station house has been damaged. (- amends 'superficial'). Superficial damage to *other* railway buildings. The line re-opened with the 7.34 Newport – Sandown on 17 May. A 5 m.p.h. restriction remained until 8.30a.m. on 31 May.
Other incidents on the same night included bombs off the track between mileposts 3 and 3¼ on the Smallbrook – Brading section which brought down the telegraph wires, causing slight damage to Shanklin Station (again!) by blast from bombs in the vicinity, and a suspected unexploded bomb near Medina Wharf.

15 July 1944
VENTNOR
VENTNOR WEST
A flying bomb exploded in the air about ½ mile from Ventnor West Station causing some damage to the buildings. The sole damage at Ventnor was one pane of broken glass in the stationmaster's house.

15 July 1944
RYDE PIER HEAD
Report received of an incident during the night of 12 July. A light Anti-Aircraft shell penetrated the roof of Brake 3rd Carriage No. 4114 making a hole about ½ inch in diameter and damaging light fittings in the compartment A. The carriage was berthed overnight at Ryde Pier Head.

ASSISTANT TO ISLE OF WIGHT MANAGER'S OFFICE

Assistant for Isle of Wight Railways
G. H. R. Gardener

Clerk 2
W. G. Dumper

Clerk 3
C. T. Bishop

Clerk 4
J. S. Reynolds

File Clerk Scale A
Mrs Janice Lakin

File Clerk Scale B
Mrs Joan Pritchard

Area Inspector 3
Ron E. Russell

Relief Signalman 1
Ray R. Draper

Assistant Relief Signalman 2
Eddie Spears

Leading Porter (DRP)
Ron G. Abbott

RYDE PIER HEAD
Stationmaster
A. G. Smith

Clerk 4
Ted Bowers
P. Hyett
R. Townson

Station Inspector 4
Harold Blundy
H. Jim Hooper

L W R A
Mrs E. Bennett

Porter
F. Budden
L. A. Corney
V. Eldridge
D. R. Heath
W. Kirkby
B. Adams
L. Playdon
E. Risdon
H. Salter
L. Patyk
J. Richards
J. Freeston
J. Savage
K. Vessey
N. Parker

Carriage Serviceman
W. Ellis
J. Bennett

Passenger Shunter
H. Yeo
George Sherlock

Ticket Collector
W. Moore
L. Smith

Porter
H. Tutton
W. Wheeler

Signalman 3
Eric Fry

Signalman 3 & Relief Signalman at Smallbrook when open
Vic Hailes

Signalman 3
J. Wells

Tram Driver
R. Roberts
F. Powell

Assistant Craneman
H. Wheeler
M. Elbourne

Ticket Collector
D. Brealey
C. Norrie

Porter
R. Elms
N. Guy
J. Lomax

RYDE ESPLANADE
Clerk 3
A. J. Carroll

Clerk 4
R. Bartrum
Norman Miller

Senior Porter
D. H. W. Cooper
V. R. J. Street

Leading Porter
Alec Kelleway

Porter
A. Bowler
T. Edmunds
W. Loraine
C. R. Hopkins

Ticket Collector
G. H. Hallam
J. Watson
F. Wendes

Porter
V. Gissing

RYDE ST. JOHN'S ROAD
Station Foreman
Les Allen

Senior Porter
P. Buck
C. Clayton

Porter
P. Beeney
D. Hughes

Signalman 3
R. Munday
Gordon Pointer
Dick Russell

Passenger Guard
Tom Courtenay
S. Jackman
H. E. Lewis
Percy Primmer
D. Williams
C. Wye
Lofty Eklund

Goods Guard
Ron Childs
Jack Forrester
W. R. Phythian
E. Storey
Jack Tharme
Wally Thrower
Sam Wells
R. Yule

BRADING
Signalman 4
Roy K. Way
Jess J. Wheeler

Leading Porter
John Jolliffe

BEMBRIDGE TOLL ROAD
Toll Collector
R. Townson
F. Williams

SANDOWN
Stationmaster
M. A. Attrill

Clerk 4
R. Wheeler
D. Slade

Signalman 3
Len Sheath
Syd. Dennett

Porter/Signalman 4
Ted Peachey

SHANKLIN
Stationmaster
Ron F. Endicott

Clerk 4
J. Amos
J. Wheeler

Signalman 4
E. Johnson

Porter/Signalman
Len Langbourne

Temporary Porter
H. G. Stockdale

WROXALL
Signalman 4
Harold A. Unstead
Richard Randall

Porter/Signalman 4
W. Lewer

VENTNOR
Clerk 4
Jack Collard
Des. G. Boynton
J. A. Veale

Signalman 4
Harold A. Fry
Sid Sartin

Porter/Signalman 3
Alec O. Widger

Porter
R. Smith
C. Punt

HAVEN STREET
Signalman 4
Terry Wright
Hughie V. White

NEWPORT
Stationmaster
A. W. G. Smith

Clerk 4
J. E. Wood
Reg. Seaman

Passenger Guard
George Francis
V. Monty Taylor

Chief Carriage Serviceman
B. R. Holbrook

Carriage Serviceman
R. H. J. Tilley
I. Chiverton

141

Station Foreman
A. F. Day

Senior Porter
E. Harris
G. Robinson

Porter
S. A. Church
Charlie Pocock
F. Parsley
O. R. Woodley
C. R. V. Putt Richardson

Junior Porter
L. J. Smith

Signalman 3
Ron Bennett
W. Day
H. Ridgeway

Relief Signalman
George Abbott

MILL HILL
Leading Porter
Arthur Darke
Horace Cade

SMITHARD'S ROAD CROSSING
Mrs M. S. Bennett

MEDINA WHARF
Goods Agent
F. W. Marsh

Dock Crane Driver
George Watson
D. Cousins
F. O'Hanlon

Checker
J. D. Turnbull

Chargeman Coal Porter
C. Kimber

Porter
C. Webb
P. Newnham
W. Eldridge
V. Croad
W. Reid
W. Hayter
J. Chessell
J. Cant
A. K. Gates
J. Sandwith
A. E. Crutcher
W. C. Reynolds
W. Saunders

Electrical Fitter
J. Harris

Fitter 3
R. Rackett

COWES
Clerk 4
Peter Griffin

Signalman 4
Herbert Watson
Larry Woodley

Porter/Signalman 4
J. Griffin

Leading Porter
A. C. Lamb

Porter
R. E. Hawkins

Assistant Leading Porter
D. Hatton

Junior Porter
B. E. Logan

Appendix Three ~ Earl Mountbatten's visit to Haven Street

Earl Mountbatten chats to Alan Blackburn, Chairman of the Isle of Wight Railway Company Board, about the future possibilities of the Isle of Wight Steam Railway. He is pictured standing outside the signalbox where he had just spent some minutes operating the signal and point levers.

Peter J. Relf

Earl Mountbatten reminiscing with Sir Peter Allen (Vice President of The Wight Locomotive Society & Chairman of ICI) and Alistair B. MacLeod (Vice President of The Wight Locomotive Society and former Assistant Divisional Operating Superintendent and Commercial Manager for the Island railways).

Peter J. Relf

Isle of Wight Steam Railway 'top brass' accompany Earl Mountbatten to his Royal Train along the platform at Haven Street. Left: Roger Silsbury Chairman of The Wight Locomotive Society and right, Alan Blackburn Chairman of The Isle of Wight Steam Railway Company. The Earl was noted to have asked at this point if he could return to the Steam Railway to see the historic No. 11 *Newport* in steam when restored. By the time this book is published this unique locomotive should be restored to full working order.

Peter J. Relf